SUSS
VILLAINS

•W•H•JOHNSON•

COUNTRYSIDE BOOKS
NEWBURY BERKSHIRE

First published 2003
© W. H. Johnson 2003

COUNTRYSIDE BOOKS
3 Catherine Road
Newbury, Berkshire

To view our complete range of books,
please visit us at
www.countrysidebooks.co.uk

ISBN 1 85306 805 5

Produced through MRM Associates Ltd., Reading
Typeset by Mac Style Ltd, Scarborough, N. Yorkshire
Printed by J.W. Arrowsmith Ltd., Bristol

Contents

INTRODUCTION

———— ❖ ————

This has been a most interesting book to write. I have constantly had to put the question to myself – what do I mean by 'villain'? Even now, with the writing complete, when I glance down the contents I am surprised at how different these men and women are and how different are my responses to them.

I cannot, for example, resist admiring Dr John Drewe for his outrageous assault on the archives of the international art world. I ought not to approve such dishonesty but I cannot at the same time avoid a sense of wonderment at how he carried his plans into action. Additionally I ought to be outraged at the shameless guile of the champagne-guzzling Horatio Bottomley but there is always some tinge of envy at the way the old fraud was able to deceive so many through his patent charm. Though his name was a byword for swindling, right to the end he pulled in suckers by the cartload. There, I've said it: I've allied myself to the bad 'uns though such a move is quite contrary to my normal disposition. Two parking tickets and a fine for speeding sums up my criminal background.

And there is Sion Jenkins. I recall the outrage I felt some years ago at this Hastings man who was imprisoned for the brutal murder of Billie-Jo, the child in his care. Added to that were the professional offences he committed when he deceived the local authority over his qualifications. But now I have read the case again in detail, studied it, considered it. I cannot deny that I am distinctly uneasy about how things have turned out for him, as I hope my observations make clear.

For good measure I have included accounts of older murders. So here is the Crowborough chicken farmer Norman Thorne, who I cannot help feel was unfortunate in his choice of girlfriend, not that that excuses how he resolved the problems she presented him with. There are also the Crumbles murderers, Field and Gray, those footloose, aimless petty thieves, and, of course, the undeniably wicked but charming John George Haigh. Charming, I hear you say? Charming? Didn't he claim to have got rid of nine people? Didn't he use an acid bath to rid himself of their corpses? True, true. But that's what is so compelling about the little dandy. He was a bright and intelligent man of untold charm. How else do you think he got away with it?

Some of the cases I am putting before you are very recent and have never before appeared in book form and I hope that readers will find them interesting and, above all, fairly told. Among these are the chapters on Nicholas van Hoogstraten, Dena Thompson and Fiona Mont whose case has yet to come before a British court.

Anyway, here's a fine gallery of villains for you, all with connections with our county. It's a county rich in so much – including villains.

W. H. Johnson

ACKNOWLEDGEMENTS

I am very grateful to those who have been able to offer me help with this book. In particular, my thanks go to former Chief Superintendents Norman Cooper, Gerry Edwards and Alan Skinner; to the Campaign for Jenkins for information on the Sion Jenkins case; and, as ever, to Paul Williams, former curator of the Black Museum, and now the man who through his Murder Files provides me with all sorts of valuable material.

I wish to thank the staff of Brighton and Hove Libraries and especially Jackie Lewis of Brighton Local Studies Library. The library services of East and West Sussex have, as ever, managed to satisfy my many needs. The staff at Eastbourne Library have been particularly helpful but then they always are.

I ought to mention an article in the Police History Society Journal (no 17, published 2002). In this, Gerry Edwards alerted readers to the fact that Elise Cameron's dismembered remains, discovered at the chicken farm in Crowborough, were taken in a wheelbarrow to the mortuary from the spot where her murderer had buried her, there being no other transport available. What would we think of that were it to happen today? How such minor details light up events of the past. I am also indebted to Gerry for the photographs of Field and Gray.

As ever, my thanks go to my wife Anne for her sorely tried patience and for her valuable commentary on each of the chapters.

For any whose copyright I have failed to trace may I apologise in advance.

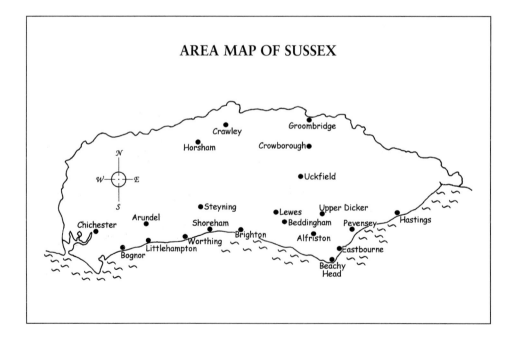

AREA MAP OF SUSSEX

PROBABLY RUTHLESS … PROBABLY VIOLENT

❀

Even if Nicholas van Hoogstraten had no responsibility for the murder of Mohammed Raja, he would qualify for entry in these pages. Sad really that it should be so, for he has so much ability, so much determination. He could have been a powerful force for good. Indeed he has demonstrated this on his extensive properties in Zimbabwe. Alas for Hoogstraten, Robert Mugabe has most recently appropriated them for his veterans, ignoring the fact that the multi-millionaire had generously provided hospitals, schools and buildings in hitherto hopelessly neglected areas. It is also said that Hoogstraten has made anonymous contributions to charities in this country too. Let it not be suggested that he does not understand human need.

It is of course this very fact, that he does understand human need, that he is aware of poverty and suffering, that makes his treatment of so many other people unforgivable. For he has rejoiced in calculated psychological warfare against the defenceless. He has been elated when his bully-boys have terrified the weak. There is no courage here. There is simply crude force and endless money.

So what makes him tick, this Sussex villain? Is he drunk with power? Perhaps. He is on record as saying, 'I have my own religion, power. I control the lives of hundreds of thousands of people just by making decisions about whether to buy or sell a business.' Is that it, the essence of Nicholas van Hoogstraten? Power, control – at any cost. Is that it? In a *World in Action* documentary he seemed to take pride in declaring, 'I'm probably ruthless and I'm probably violent.' He does not care that you know this. You can do nothing to him. That is what he has so frequently implied publicly.

Perhaps the signs were always there, back in his Shoreham boyhood, back in the days when, a relatively friendless boy, he persuaded another youth to steal a typewriter for him. Typical that, distant and manipulative, he should engage someone else to do the dirty work, for this seems to be a continuing feature of many Hoogstraten operations. As a teenager he was on probation after the first of his several subsequent brushes with the law. His parents were concerned enough to believe that he needed to be straightened out. They sent him to sea. Not before the mast, of course. He became a lift boy on a cruise ship to the West Indies. And here it was that the van Hoogstraten empire began in earnest, though even as a 14 year old schoolboy he had been a serious reader of the *Financial Times* when his fellow pupils were just at the point of giving up the *Eagle*.

And it was in the West Indies that the lift boy saw the opportunities. While the passengers were ashore visiting old colonial forts and sugar plantations, sipping rum and listening to calypso singers, Nicholas van Hoogstraten was buying land. All those passengers were sitting on a goldmine but only the lift boy realised it. And the money? Where did that come from? Years earlier his father had given him a very valuable stamp collection. The boy turned it into silver. West Indian land prices rocketed and the silver turned into gold when Hoogstraten sold up.

At the age of 18 the budding tycoon bought land in Zimbabwe. He was soon to establish business interests in the Bahamas. And, he had started to invest in his south-east coast properties.

By the time he was 21 Hoogstraten was a millionaire, a 'wunderkind'. Where would his business acumen lead him next? He had the ability to have taken over major national and international companies. He could have become a significant political figure. It is impossible to work out why, with such undeniable potential, he was content to become master of a grubby, dishonourable trade.

At 22 Hoogstraten had 300 run-down properties in Brighton, all of them bought dirt-cheap. He would eventually own 2,000. In these early days, when he was acknowledged as Britain's youngest millionaire, he was also a nightclub owner and partner in a Brighton fashion boutique. It has never been difficult for Hoogstraten to fall out with his partners. He did so at the boutique after the venture failed and he and David Braunstein were in dispute over money. Hoogstraten is on record as saying, 'I go for direct personal retribution.' In August 1968, to prove this point, to indicate that he was not a man to be trifled with, Hoogstraten's minions visited Braunstein's house and lobbed a hand grenade through the ground floor window. The man, his wife and their six children who were upstairs, were mercifully uninjured.

Nicholas van Hoogstraten, standing in front of Hamilton Palace which was to be 'fit for a king'. (John Connor Press Associates)

Hoogstraten, 25 years old, was sentenced to four years' imprisonment for this outrage. In the dock at Lewes he was unperturbed. His arrogance prompted the judge to comment that the defendant was 'a sort of self-imagined devil who thinks he is an emissary of Beelzebub'.

Several years later in a television interview, saturnine and rather elegant, he was still unrepentant. The years had not caused him to reflect on his actions. His view of the incident, which the most generous might have put down to immaturity, had not changed with time. There was no sense of guilt or shame. His moral standards are of his own design. 'I think it is marvellous,' Hoogstraten had said at the time of his trial. 'The bastard owed me money.' He continued to hold that position.

In the interview he asserted that he saw nothing wrong in attacking an opponent with a grenade. Could he think of no other way of punishing the man? Yes, he would have liked to have had 'his bollocks chopped off'. He was serious about that, he said. 'Make the punishment fit the crime.'

It might have been expected that when released from jail Hoogstraten would at least have been circumspect. Not so. The accountant who had helped run the thriving property business was now adjudged to have swindled the firm of £14,000 in Hoogstraten's absence. Take him to court? Not a chance. Punishment was visited on the culprit, Hoogstraten-style. He was picked up by Hoogstraten and two other men outside a bank in North Street, Brighton. He was bundled into the boot of a Rolls-Royce and taken to France where, existing on a diet of sardines for a year, he was forced to work off his debt. Nor did he try to escape. There were threats of what would happen to him and his family if he did so. This was Hoogstraten's law.

It was about this time that Hoogstraten bought the High Cross estate near Uckfield. Here he employed precisely those methods of getting rid of his unwanted tenants that he employed across the Brighton slum empire. The elderly occupants at High Cross were terrorised by thugs employed by Hoogstraten, their lives made a total misery. There was no mercy shown. On a daily basis his 'winklers' as he called them threatened the occupants, cut their telephone lines, cut off their water and electricity, did everything to destroy the lives of decent, respectable people. Like others faced by such intimidation they left in distress. But there is an immature quality of spite in all of this, the malicious child's delight in discomfiting others.

In the course of many years Hoogstraten had bought scores of cheap properties at auction in Brighton. Sometimes he purchased whole streets. He subsequently sold them with vacant possession after refurbishing them with government grants. The profits were enormous. But there were usually existing tenants, often on low rents. The lives of these inconvenient people were made unbearable. Roof leaks were not repaired; power was cut off and not restored for days; disorderly all-night parties by 'neighbours from Hell' were encouraged; on occasion the staircases to upper floors were removed. Hoogstraten has said that some tenants who complained met with 'accidents'. There were forcible evictions during which personal belongings were destroyed. How amused he was when hippies had no choice but to jump from the second storey windows to escape the German Shepherd dogs his 'winklers' took into a building. In 1974 he was fined £3,000 after an especially fierce eviction which became known as the 'Battle of Brighton'. But such fines were paltry and worth it for the entertainment he derived. 'It's great fun', he told the *Evening Argus*, 'and there isn't a thing they can do about it.' Hoogstraten has justified his actions with as specious an argument as he can summon up. 'Tenants are filth by their very nature,' he says. 'What kind of person is a tenant? A person with no self-respect. I don't look after tenants. Why should I? One looks after the building, looks after one's asset.'

Mrs Jackie Hope was surprised to find two men in her garden one day and asked who they were. 'I am the owner,' Hoogstraten told her. 'Get out of here.' When she told him that she would go to her solicitor, the other man, Robert Knapp, accompanying his boss, replied, 'You won't need a solicitor. You'll need a doctor. And you'll be in a wheelchair.' And Hoogstraten spat in her face. Questioned about this on television Hoogstraten admitted spitting. He was not proud of it, he said, but it had had the desired effect. Perhaps it is not a surprising response from a man who has described women as 'a pain in the arse,' his own mother as 'a whining cow.' Knapp moved into the flat below Mrs Hope, and made her life a misery. Fortunately and much to her relief, after six months he was given a 13 year jail sentence for armed robbery.

In 1991 Hoogstraten successfully prevented the leaseholders of Palmeira Square in Hove from buying the freehold. They had originally thought that they had bought the freehold but then it was found that two of the flats were registered to companies in which Hoogstraten had an interest. Litigation, thanks to Hoogstraten, was prolonged and complex. One of his companies allegedly sold the lease of the broom cupboard in the basement to another company with which he was associated. This simply tangled up the legal process and added to the residents' legal fees. Hoogstraten broke no law in this case but there was meanness of spirit about the whole matter. It does seem like purposeless bullying, the brutal, almost childish, exercise of power. The seven residents were left with costs of £200,000.

In 1980 Hoogstraten was fined for unpaid tax and asked to stump up £5.3 million. It was paid within two years. The *Guinness Book of Records* identifies this as the highest ever fine levied by the Inland Revenue.

About this time plans for Hamilton Palace on the site of the old house at High Cross were drawn up. The building, with its copper dome and its interior of marble and oak, was to be larger than Buckingham Palace, was to be fit for a king. It was to house Hoogstraten's collection of art and antiquities. The east wing was to serve as a mausoleum, for Hoogstraten's tomb, sealed up for 5,000 years, away from the eyes of the 'peasants', whom we take to be the author of this book, its readers, and 99.9 per cent of the population.

It may be, however, that Hamilton Palace will not be completed. Since building began in 1985 an estimated £9 million has been paid out. It is now suggested that perhaps another £25 million will be required for its completion. Since 2000, legal problems have brought work to a halt and the site is said to be deteriorating.

Despite the hold-up, Hoogstraten conducted a struggle against 'perverts, anarchists and the dirty mac brigade' as he has labelled the Ramblers' Association. They wished to use a long-established footpath crossing his land but he refused to have such 'riff-raff' traipsing over his property. The path was blocked; there were court hearings. Happily, however, while Hoogstraten has languished in prison, the ramblers have won their case and the footpath is once again open.

There are many other matters, too, not to be dealt with here in any detail, to be added to the tally. These include: in 1978 the barricading of a nursing home, its twelve occupants, all elderly, deprived of lighting and heating; in 1990 the fire in the flat in Hove's Palmeira Avenue in which five people died; the fine for contempt after saying of a judge, 'I'll get him in 10 years' time.'

Hoogstraten has said that at one time he was encouraged by the police to rid Hove of its many drug addicts. He claimed to have used his usual methods, happy to send them eastwards to Brighton where there was 'a much lower class of occupant'.

Enough then on this curriculum vitae to place Nicholas van Hoogstraten in any gallery of Sussex villains. But there is more.

On 2nd July 1999 Mohammed Raja was murdered in the hallway of his home in Sutton. A notorious Brighton slum landlord, his properties were neglected and over the years he had been severely fined by the local authority for health and safety violations. Raja had borrowed money from Hoogstraten for some of his ventures in return for which he had handed over some property deeds. Raja was paying back his debt in weekly instalments but there arose a disagreement over the amount still owed. Can these two businessmen have been keeping the sums in their heads? Raja estimated his debt to be in the region of £200,000: Hoogstraten arrived at a different figure. He was asking for £600,000. Legal action followed and trickled on for six years. Then, Raja found evidence that he had been defrauded by Hoogstraten and declared his intention to take the case to the High Court. Now Hoogstraten faced demands of £5.8 million and the prospect of a prison sentence. Could he then be the instigator of Raja's murder?

Certainly the dying Raja, with stab wounds to the chest and a gunshot wound to his head, was heard by his two grandsons, Rizvan and Waheed, to gasp out his last words, 'They are Hoogstraten's men. They have hit me.' This was a huge lead for the police. Hoogstraten had every motive for ridding himself of the man who might land him in prison. But there was no evidence and after being interviewed Hoogstraten, cool and assured as ever, was released. But the police knew Hoogstraten well, knew about his enforcers, the 'winklers' who had made the lives of so many tenants an unbearable misery. Hadn't he once in a television interview referred to these men, smirking as he spoke, 'We have people we call on from time to time'? Perhaps it would pay the police to concentrate on some of these.

Of one thing the police were certain. Mohammed Raja was not the victim of professional hitmen. Amateurism was written all over the murder. The two men, disguised as gardeners – one carried a gardening fork, the other a sawn-off shotgun hidden under his coat – had met Raja in the hallway of his home. His grandsons, both young adults, who were upstairs at the time, heard shouting and then shots. They ran downstairs to where Raja lay fatally wounded. The young men were unable to prevent the escape of the killers, who ran from the house and drove off in a white van.

Amateurish murder or not, the police had no other indication of whom they sought. They were convinced, however, that Hoogstraten was in some way involved. All they had were samples of blood, not all of it from Raja, at the murder scene.

The investigation progressed slowly. They began to wonder about Robert Knapp, recently released from prison. Remember Knapp? He was the 'winkler' who had made Mrs Jackie Hope's life such a misery ten years earlier. And his mother was now living in a cottage on High Cross estate where Hoogstraten was building his palace.

Another name came up too. One of Knapp's associates, bank robber David Croke, was also recently out after a 20 year stretch. He and Knapp, the police thought, might be involved. Yet there was no evidence against either man. Then, in February 2001 Croke was arrested by Suffolk police on a minor drugs charge. Now there was the legal right for police to take DNA samples. And these matched the blood found nearly two years earlier in Raja's house. Croke was arrested in Brighton. And as one thing leads to another, so Croke led to Robert Knapp.

The police studied mobile phone records to track the relationship between Croke and Knapp. They had been released within weeks of each other in the early summer of 1999. Between then and the day of the murder they had phoned each other frequently. After the murder there was no further communication. The mobile phone data also showed that on the day of the murder they drove round the M25 to Crayford in Kent. The police then discovered that both men arrived in Kent with superficial burns. The white van was found, burnt out, not far from Crayford.

Croke was charged with the murder of Mohammed Raja. Knapp at the time was away in Ireland. And now Hoogstraten fell into the net. He had seemed invulnerable. The police, though sure of his involvement, had nothing to charge him with. But then they re-read the notes of Hoogstraten's interview eighteen months earlier. And something clicked. There was something there, the significance of which only now occurred to the investigating officers. In his interview in which Hoogstraten had come over as arrogantly confident, he had asked 'How did he miss with the first shot?' The first shot? That was it. Those were the words which tied Hoogstraten in with the killing. The first shot. It was not public knowledge that the first shot had hit the ceiling. How did Hoogstraten know that more than one shot had been fired? He could only know if either Knapp or Croke had told him. He had given himself away. The man who in the past had bragged that he was too clever to be caught was arrested at his office in the Courtlands Hotel in Hove. When Knapp returned from Ireland in September 2001, he too was arrested.

Then came information from another slum landlord, Abou Hamdan. He made a statement saying that Hoogstraten talked about finding a hitman to kill Raja. This was powerful stuff for the prosecution.

Next, Hoogstraten's 18 year old girlfriend, Tanaka Sali, went to the police, her cheek badly swollen. Hoogstraten, out on bail, had beaten her up for seeing another man and had thrown her out of the house. And Hell hath no fury ... She described how Knapp had been introduced to her as 'one of my hitmen'.

On 16th April 2002, the trial of Hoogstraten, Knapp and Croke began at the Old Bailey. The case against Hoogstraten was circumstantial. Admittedly there was a motive but Raja had other enemies; the sum of money that had caused the breach between the two men was regarded by Hoogstraten as 'trifling'; clippings relating to the murder found in Hoogstraten's house were scarcely damning; the error relating to 'the first shot' could be explained away by a smart counsel; a record of payments to Knapp amounting to £7,000 was not necessarily proof of a contract killing. The defence claimed that there was no evidence against Hoogstraten and that he was simply 'guilty by association'.

As the trial developed there was bad news for the prosecution. Abou Hamdan fled to Beirut, refusing to give evidence. The jury was not allowed to hear what he had told the police.

Then Tanaka Sali, dressed in expensive new clothes, turned up in court. She told the judge that she had decided not to appear in the witness box. 'I'd rather go to prison than end up dead,' she said, preferring to face the wrath of the court rather than Hoogstraten's. 'Hamdan is as good as dead,' she said. She was not going to risk her life. The jury heard nothing about the statement she had made.

The case for the prosecution was increasingly shaky until Hoogstraten, against counsel's advice, insisted on giving evidence It was the only way he could lose the trial, they told him. But overweening pride urged him into the witness box.

In the box, Hoogstraten could not conceal his own nature. No, he said, he was not a violent man. But extracts from television programmes were shown in which he had said, in that familiarly supercilious manner of his, that he had '… a few violent associates … people we can call on …' Yes, he said, laughing as he spoke, people had been forced to jump out of second storey windows. Oblivious of the impression he was creating, he revealed himself as a man consumed by his own significance. In consequence, the jury concluded that he had sent his two henchmen to frighten Raja out of proceeding with the fraud case. But Knapp and Croke had either not understood what it was they were intended to do or their enterprise was botched. Both men were sentenced to life imprisonment for murder.

Hoogstraten's sentencing was delayed for several weeks for psychiatric reports. On 25th October 2002 the court heard that he was not suffering from any mental incapacity but that he displayed 'narcissistic' and 'paranoid' personality traits. Mr Justice Newman sentenced him to ten years' imprisonment 'on the basis that you were the instigator of a terrifying piece of intimidation which was designed to convey a threat to Mr Raja that he would be caused really serious bodily harm or be killed'. The judge went on to observe about Hoogstraten, 'He never takes any responsibility for the things he has done. The reports show he always thinks he is in the right.'

In December 2002 the Raja family were awarded £5,000,000 against Hoogstraten for alleged property fraud. Now after the High Court appointed a sequestrator to seize his assets it was suggested that he faced financial ruin. Hoogstraten was expected to regain what remained of his property only when the Raja family had received damages and when other debts had been paid off.

Yet there is no doubt that there is still a powerful Hoogstraten empire, cunningly concealed in a myriad offshore accounts of Byzantine complexity, and this is likely to survive until his release in perhaps 2008. In July 2003, the Appeal judges quashed the conviction for manslaughter and ordered a retrial. This is likely to take place in 2004. Hoogstraten has been refused bail and is remanded in custody. Still a multi-millionaire, he will in the meantime be a king over the water, making decisions about what occurs right to the furthest boundaries of his territories. He will reach out through his prison bars ...

A Very Bubbly Lady

———— ❁ ————

When Richard Thompson turned up at Worthing Hospital on the night of 2nd January 2000 he was treated for deep cuts on the forehead and shoulder. He had five stitches to a wound above his left eye, three to a wound over the right eye and seven to the shoulder injuries. His wife – his 'soon-to-be-ex-wife' as he referred to her – had come at him, he said, with a metal baseball bat and a knife. He'd been lucky to escape.

The blood found on the door, radiator, tiles, floor and walls of the bathroom testified to the struggle that had taken place. The bedroom carpet was bloodied, too, as was the baseball bat, the kitchen knife and a black leather belt. Two days later when he was visited by police at his Rustington home, Thompson was still visibly shaken. His wife had taken him quite by surprise, he said. It was the last thing he'd bargained for. Husbands don't expect to be attacked by their wives, wielding such weapons. And especially when they are anticipating something totally different. They'd taken a bath together, he told the police, and then she'd told him she had 'a surprise' for him. Did he remember that little game they played several days earlier? He did. It was the game where he was not allowed to touch her. Well, she'd told him, they were going to play it again. But this time, she said, she was going to be much stricter.

Minutes later Richard lay on the bathroom floor bound with brown masking tape and a leather belt and with a towel over his head. And waited … Some surprise. He felt two savage blows to the head. She had swung the baseball bat at him. But he had managed to twist away and had scrambled to his feet. And she, pursuing him, slipped on the blood pouring from his head. It was his chance and, struggling free of his bonds, he managed to overpower her. Years earlier he had learnt martial arts and this experience now served him well.

The struggle over, he had calmed her down and had asked her to telephone her parents. They arrived from London three hours later and took Richard to hospital.

And this is one account of what happened at Willow Cottage that the jury heard at Lewes Crown Court in August 2000 when Dena Thompson was tried for the attempted murder of her husband.

Dena for her part described matters differently. Her version denied any suggestion of bondage. She was sitting on the bed in her knickers while the bath was running and Richard, using a kitchen knife, was trying to mend a roller blind in the bathroom at the same time. They had had an argument, a serious argument. And he had snapped, she said. He'd come through from the bathroom brandishing the 12-inch knife. She'd grabbed the baseball bat to defend herself and had hit him with it twice. But he was too strong, she told the jury. He'd grabbed hold of the bat and had thrown it into the kitchen. He had overpowered her, climbed on top of her, his thumb pushing into her left eye. 'I thought he was going to kill me,' she said. But in the struggle he had dropped the knife. 'I saw the knife on the right-hand side. I picked it up, brought it across and cut his right arm, then threw the knife under the bed. He brought his fist up as though he was going to smash my face in.'

Unexpectedly, Dena said, he then calmed down, stood up and told her to clean up the blood in the bathroom and on the bedroom carpet. She had offered to call an ambulance but instead he asked her to call her parents. Her father had taken him to Worthing Hospital.

The jury found Dena Thompson's story more believable and she was found not guilty of attempted murder but other factors introduced in this lurid case were to lead her to prison – and not for the first time. The story was astonishing.

In October 1998 Richard Thompson, a 42 year old security official employed as a British Telecom investigator, responded to a 'lonely hearts' advertisement in the local free newspaper, *Friday Ad*. At that time, according to Joanna Greenwood, her defence

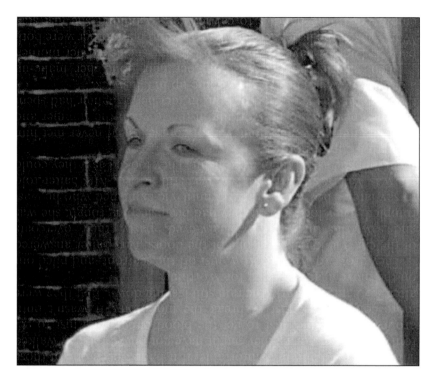

Dena Thompson. (John Connor Press Associates)

counsel, Dena 'was grossly overweight, jobless and virtually penniless with a child to keep.' Richard was to say in court that 'she was a very bubbly lady. There was not much physical attraction at first but her character was attractive'. So before Christmas she and her young son moved into his bungalow.

Then came the tragic news. Dena told Richard that she had been diagnosed with breast and ovarian cancer. His response was to take an early retirement package of £36,000 to stay at home to care for her. But there was a future the couple told themselves. In April 1999 they went off to Florida where they married romantically on the beach. They investigated the possibility of moving to Florida permanently and in the course of 1999 they made several visits there. They never finalised a house purchase although Richard had handed over a £3,000 deposit on one property. He had an idea of buying a boat and becoming a fisherman. Dena knew someone who could help; she knew just the man and tried on several occasions to fix a meeting between him and Richard. Unfortunately, she told him, the go-between was working undercover for the FBI and could not be contacted.

And then the good news ... Dena told Richard that now that she was happily married and knew that he was not after her money, she felt able to tell him ... she had won a considerable amount of money on the National Lottery. Between £250,000 and £300,000.

And the bad news ... at the moment the money was in a Jersey bank account, Dena said. And it was proving difficult to release. Just a temporary hold-up, she said. You know these Channel Island banks, what they're like. And hold-up or no, it did not stop them from refurbishing the bungalow or from taking foreign holidays or from indulging themselves with 'little luxuries' and a 'few extras'. And Richard trusted her, one hundred per cent. She was, he said, his 'soul mate'.

But Richard was to have increasing doubts. Why was the lottery money in a Jersey account? Fine, all right, Dena had a reason for that. But why was it taking so long to transfer the money to a mainland account? She explained the reason perfectly logically. But week after week went by, month after month. There was something decidedly odd about this. Richard couldn't understand it, no matter what she said. It just did not seem right. And had she really been a college lecturer? And an antiques dealer? There were just some worrying little things that did not always add up.

And so to the night of 2nd January. Dena's account differed totally from Richard's. They had argued about money, she said. He was mending the blind and she was sitting on the bed. Richard had wanted to go to Florida the following day. He had boasted to his friends that he would be fishing there on 4th January, his birthday. And she, exasperated, told him that he could not go. She confessed. There was no money. It was all spent up. She had defrauded him. There was no lottery win. There was no 'go-between' in America who would fit him up with a fishing job. The deposit paid on a Florida property? Forget it. It had gone into one of her accounts and it had been spent.

And hearing all this, he had come at her. That was what Dena told the court. She made no bones about it. She admitted to seven charges of fraud. But she did not accept that she had tried to murder her husband.

Philip Katz, for the prosecution, however, claimed that she feared that Richard had discovered that she had squandered his money, that she had forged credit cards in his name, that she had lied to him about having cancer and that in desperation she had tried to kill him. It was the imminent discovery of what she had done which had led to her to try to kill her husband as he lay awaiting his 'surprise' on the bathroom floor.

The defence counsel, Joanna Greenberg, did not deny her client's rampant dishonesty. But she contested that Dena would never have attempted to commit murder. It would be too 'unprofessional'. Dena Thompson didn't go in for such clumsy methods. She was too intelligent for that. If she had intended to kill Richard she would have found a way which did not implicate her. Her client was a consummate liar, Ms Greenberg said. 'If she tells you today is Friday you would probably want to check in your newspaper for the truth. She isn't an honest woman. But despite an appalling record of dishonesty she has never been violent.'

Appalling record for dishonesty? Absolutely. Dena admitted that she planned to find a fishing job for Richard in Florida. In his absence she had intended to sell the house and those of his shares she had not yet had her hands on. She would then just disappear.

Dena Thompson was a serial fraudster. The court heard that she had had a string of lovers whom she had over the years relieved of considerable sums of money. Several of them preferred not to become involved with police enquiries – they had wives; they were still paying off the debts which had come to light after she had left them. But two ex-lovers did make statements.

One of them had met Dena in 1997 through an advertisement in *Friday Ad* just as Richard Thompson would do the following year. Within three weeks she had moved in with him. He had felt sorry for her after she told him that she was being harassed by a man who had attacked her three years earlier. After this she told him she was dying of cancer. She had business connections in America, she told him, and she invited him on a business trip to Orlando, all expenses paid for by her company. He discovered later that she had intercepted his credit card Pin number in the post and that the money for the trip had been paid for out of his own account. In all he lost £4,404.

In 1998 a second man met Dena in Worthing where she was working in a fabric shop. She was very friendly and offered him free off-cuts of material if he would take her out for a drink. It was the beginning of a brief relationship. There were the usual heart-rending tales. Her father had died recently of throat cancer, she told him. And she too suffered from the same ailment; she would be dead by Christmas. But within weeks the man began to feel uneasy about her behaviour and their partnership ended. Fortunately, she took no more than £500 from his bank account.

It transpired that Dena Thompson's history of deception went back several years. In 1995 she had been convicted at Chichester of stealing £26,000 from customer accounts at the Arundel branch of the Woolwich Building Society where she worked. She had tried to implicate her first husband, Lee Wyatt, by tricking him into writing a series of letters in which he incriminated himself. At the trial, Judge Eric Wrintmore described her as 'one of the most fluent liars I have ever come across.' Convicted on seven counts of theft and two of forgery she was sentenced to 18 months' imprisonment.

Yes, Dena Thompson's record was appalling but Joanna Greenberg denied that her client had attempted to murder her husband, Richard Thompson. The charge was his invention, his way of getting back at the wife who had admitted to defrauding him. In fact, he was as bad as Dena. He had been after her money. But he was not as clever as his wife.

'Do you think he would have shown the slightest interest in her if he knew the truth?' Ms Greenberg asked. 'He saw Mrs Thompson as a golden goose, even before he was told of the lottery money.' But she admitted that her client was the author of her own misfortune. 'She played with fire and she got burned.'

In August 2000, Dena Thompson was jailed at Lewes Crown Court for three years and nine months on 15 counts of deception.

Judge Anthony Scott-Gall said that she had used 'lies and deceit on a grand and convincing scale ... you stole property from vulnerable men, all of whom in their way had become enamoured with you and Mr Thompson went so far as to marry you. You are someone who is irredeemably dishonest and driven by a desire to defraud people of their property.'

Detective Constable Sean McDonald who worked on the attempted murder case is on record as describing her as 'one of the most dangerous people I have ever met ... She is cunning, conniving, calculating and contemptuous. In 15 years on the job I have never come across anyone quite like Dena Thompson.'

And the story does not quite end there. But we need first to go back to 1991, shortly after Dena and her first husband, Lee Wyatt, separated. In that year, after what was described as a whirlwind romance, Julian Webb, a local newspaper advertising manager, married Dena at Chichester registry office. It later transpired that this was a bigamous marriage.

On his 31st birthday, after three years of marriage, Webb was found dead in bed at his home in Yapton. He had taken an overdose of paracetamol and dothiepin, an antidepressant. At the time there were suspicions about his death but the police found no evidence of foul play. At the inquest, however, the coroner said that he was satisfied Julian Webb would never have considered taking his own life and an open verdict was recorded.

Immediately after the trial for the attempted murder of Richard Thompson, Sussex police renewed their interest in Webb's death. In October 2001 his body was exhumed. In April 2002 an official investigation into the case was reopened. At the time of writing this account it is not known what may yet unfold.

MASTER OF CHAOS – OR CHARLATAN?

───────────❀───────────

Only when she was certain that the visitor was gone and not lurking nearby, did Kathleen Neuberg leave the house. She was terrified. She knew from her husband about the awful and awesome powers of the man who not an hour before had called at Vine Cottage and asked for Victor. She had no need to ask him to introduce himself. Though she had never met the caller she knew him at once. She had heard Victor speak of him often enough, had heard of his fear that one day he would be tracked down to Steyning, that one day he would again come face to face with the man whom he had once called Master. Even though it was now thirteen years since the two men had last seen each other in 1914, Victor had always feared a visit from the man who had cursed him. Their parting had been an experience which marked him for life. But then their association had lasted nearly twenty years and that too had marked Victor, had scored his mind, scarred his soul.

And now this horrifying figure from the past had appeared at the cottage door.

'Victor Neuberg,' the caller had said, his manner domineering as if he were speaking to an inferior. 'I wish to see him.'

And Kathleen had known immediately who it was. She had seen newspaper photographs of the man often enough. There was no mistaking that enormous shaven head, that puffy face with the fierce, disturbing eyes. But despite all she knew of her visitor, she did not allow herself to show any weakness. She held firm.

'He's not here,' she had answered.

And she had consistently made the same reply in the face of continuing questioning from this man who to her personified evil.

The man's growing anger, his tone of voice, his fearsome expression and the very menace that exuded from him had no obvious effect on her.

'He's not here,' she repeated time after time as the visitor in his rage dashed his stick against the path. But she would not yield and finally he left.

Only then did Kathleen, shaken and fearful, leave the house, taking the track up to the Downs where Victor was spending the day walking. Finally she met him and told him of the visit. He was terrified at the news.

'It was Aleister, you're sure?' he asked. Perhaps she had been mistaken.

It was Aleister, all right. No doubt about it. Now, after all these years, Aleister had come for him. God knows what might happen now. To be found here when he had begun to think that perhaps he was safe ... and now after all this time Aleister Crowley had come. Crowley, named by the press as the Worst Man in Britain, the Wickedest Man in the World; Crowley, the man held by some to be the Antichrist, the man whose own mother, a profoundly committed member of the Plymouth Brotherhood, had likened to the Great Beast 666 of the *Book of Revelations*. And now he had at last sought out Victor Neuberg, his one-time acolyte and lover, one of those very few to break away from Crowley, one of those rare beings who had dared to leave the debauched magic world of the man who called himself Frater Perdurabo; The Supreme and Holy Baphomet; The Secret Wanderer of the Waste; The Guardian of the Flame; Mega Therion; and ultimately, when he became as near to a god as is possible, Ipsissimus. Crowley claimed to be all of these, knew he was all of these, for he was the possessor of knowledge not known to other humans. Had not that discarnate intelligence, Aiwass, dictated the new law of mankind to him over three days in Cairo? Was not the true religion that of Shaitan, the true founder of mankind, whose role had been misrepresented by Christians? It was all there in Crowley's *Book of the Law* in which he enjoined his followers, 'Do what thou wilt'. Crowley himself had been raised to godlike status.

A god? A man in touch with gods? With demons? With the Devil? These were the claims of Aleister Crowley who in the first

Aleister Crowley

half of the 20th century was both the epitome of human depravity and in the eyes of some the greatest exponent of the Black Arts of his time. Crowley proclaimed himself to be the channel of communication between the occult intelligences of superhuman knowledge and power against what he held to be the pernicious and false doctrines of Christianity. A man of frightening power, Crowley pursued a so-called religion marked by depraved rituals and yet he was followed by many convinced by his claims.

Not all of course could remain loyal to Crowley, given the excesses of drugs, dissolute sexual behaviour and alcohol which fuelled their enthusiasms. It was well enough known that in the course of his life many members of his Order had come to sad ends. There was, for example, Brother Omnia Pro Veritate, Professor of Applied Mathematics at Bloemfontein University. His real name was Norman Mudd ('My name is Mudd,' he would introduce himself). He had fallen from grace, had been cursed by the Beast and had committed suicide. Then there was Raoul Loveday who, trying out some of his master's obscure religious rituals, ended up with his body scarred all over with self-inflicted wounds. He had died of gastro-enteritis. His wife Betty had hated the insane life in which she had found herself. After Raoul's death she told the newspapers how Master Therion – Crowley – had invited them to eat black puddings of goats' blood and to drink the blood of a sacrificial cat. This is what, she claimed, had poisoned her husband. She told too how at the Sicilian villa at Cefalu, where Crowley had established his Abbey of Thelema, his children, neglected and half starved, had witnessed orgies, the grossest scenes of debauchery, erotic ceremonies, Black Masses. And there were the unhappy women in his entourage, all of them used and abused, yet rejoicing in the names Crowley had given them – The Ape of Thoth; The Dog-Headed Hermes; The Camel; The Cat; The Monkey. At least five of his countless former mistresses – his 'Scarlet Women' as Crowley called them – had committed suicide, as had male lovers and friends who had fallen out of favour. The Master's first two wives were in insane asylums.

And now Crowley had come to Steyning. There was so much history in their relationship, too much ever to be forgotten of a nightmare world.

When he was a 20 year old student at Trinity, Cambridge, Neuberg had first met Crowley, eight years his senior and already head of his own occult Order of the Silver Star. It was then that Crowley, a man of independent financial means, already dissipated by drugs and drink, initiated the younger man into the rites of his creed of sexual magic. Neuberg had been entranced by the charismatic Crowley, a legendary mountaineer who as a pupil at Eastbourne College had scaled Beachy Head on several occasions and who was later to go on to conquer some of the world's most demanding mountains. But Crowley was more than that. He was a profound philosopher and had an encyclopaedic knowledge of Eastern religions as well as necromancy. He was a good painter, a competent novelist and a well above average poet. He was a brilliant chess player, the one-time secretary of Eastbourne Chess Society. From his earliest years he was a drug addict, taking alarmingly massive quantities of cocaine, opium, ether, hashish and heroin. And he was undoubtedly obsessed by sex and sexual practices.

At Boleskine House on Loch Ness, totally dominated by Crowley, Neuberg was initiated into the Order after a series of bizarre ceremonies and ordeals, culminating in his having to sleep naked for seven nights on a litter of gorse. The rituals which Crowley had devised for the Order were weird and frightening. Drugs were frequently used to induce trance-like states. Others had effects similar to those of LSD. In a trance in Dorset Neuberg took the part of Mars and believed himself to have been possessed by the god. It was during this trance, according to Crowley, that Neuberg predicted the 1912 Balkan War and the Great War.

For the next few years Crowley, Neuberg and a collection of followers travelled through Europe and Africa where Crowley continued his practice of powerful magic using Neuberg and other men and women sexually as mediums for the gods. In the notorious so-called 'Paris Working' where Jupiter and Hermes were called on, the ritual culminated in the most depraved sexual acts between Crowley and Neuberg. In the Algerian Sahara both men experienced visions and Crowley was said to have conjured up the demon Choronzon, the epitome of all disharmony and confusion, in the form of a naked savage who broke through the magic protective circle that Crowley had laid down by spells. The demon rushed at Neuberg, hit him and nearly destroyed him. Crowley, incensed at Neuberg's reactions, claimed to have metamorphosed him into a camel.

Certainly, Neuberg's shambling gait and hangdog appearance annoyed Crowley who feared that the natives might not take him seriously. Neuberg was ordered to shave his head so that only two tufts were left on the temples and these were twisted into horns. From then on, when in Africa Neuberg was introduced as a demon trained by Crowley to act as his familiar spirit. In his *Confessions* Crowley writes: 'The more eccentric and horrible Neuberg appeared, the more insanely and grotesquely he behaved, the more he inspired the inhabitants with respect for the Magician who had mastered so fantastic and fearful a genie.'

Let it not be thought that Victor Neuberg was totally innocent in any of this mixture of depravity, mumbo-jumbo and genuine magical practice. It is said that Crowley turned down Neuberg's proposal that they abduct, rape, murder and dismember a young woman and offer her remains to the Egyptian god Thoth.

But even the most loyal lovers and enthusiastic followers can come eventually to realise the awfulness of the situation in which they find themselves. In 1912 a woman who was having an affair with Neuberg committed suicide after The Master, for his own reasons, interfered with and then ended the relationship. That was one major reason for Neuberg's loss of faith. And then of course he began to suspect that Crowley, having spent the enormous fortune he had inherited at the age of 21, was now using his Magick (Crowley's spelling of the word!) not for the attainment of esoteric knowledge but in order to raise cash for himself. Crowley, it seemed to his disillusioned follower, was duping people, especially wealthy neurotic women, for cash. Even so, it took Neuberg two years before he dared to abandon Crowley. But he left with terror in his soul, a nervous wreck, ritually cursed and genuinely fearing the power of Crowley's spells.

By 1919, after war service, Victor Neuberg settled in his aunt's home at Vine Cottage which seemed a safe haven. He set up his own publishing firm, Vine Press, and here he wrote poetry. Several of his poems are about Chanctonbury Ring, that haunted place with associations with the Devil and witchcraft. One of these poems describes the sacrificial burning of a youth by Druids.

Then Kathleen Goddard came into Neuberg's life and he married her in 1921. Three years later, their son Victor was born. Life now must have seemed safe, though despite his talent, success in the literary world was elusive. His association with the notorious Crowley deterred many who would otherwise have acknowledged his merits. Nevertheless, friends from the cultural world that he naturally inhabited visited him at Steyning. Singer Paul Robeson, actress Tallullah Bankhead, writer Gertrude Stein were among those who came to Vine Cottage.

And then one day in 1927 Aleister Crowley came knocking at the door, looking for his acolyte.

Is it any wonder that Victor Neuberg and his wife, terrified at the reappearance of Crowley, left Steyning at once and went into hiding? The two men never met again. Perhaps Crowley simply abandoned the idea of pursuing Neuberg. But for his part, Neuberg would never drive from his mind the experiences to which Crowley introduced him. Together, high on drugs and drink taken in the course of magical rites, they claimed to have visited other terrible places quite beyond normal human experience. And throughout all the years since leaving The Master, Neuberg never forgot his terrible passage through whirlpools, through vast swirling abysses, through the haunts of terrifying phantoms. Here were dreams of meeting the archangel Gabriel; dreams of crucifixion by two angels; dreams of the Red Giant who hacked him to pieces; dreams of the virgin princess who had his hands and feet chopped off before he was sacrificed on an altar. These were the most terrible nightmare visions that stayed with Neuberg, always convinced that he really had been transported under Crowley's spells to such wildernesses of despair.

Even so, afraid though he was, in 1930 in the magazine *Freethinker* Neuberg praised Crowley's autobiography as one of the greatest ever published and likened his former lover to other great writers of genius. Perhaps such soft words were enough to satisfy any vengeful feelings that Crowley still entertained.

Victor Neuberg died in 1940, modestly successful as a poet and publisher, the man who had first put the writing of Dylan Thomas in print. His mentor, the undeniably wicked and self-absorbed Crowley, penniless now, lasted until 1947 when he died in a Hastings boarding house, Netherwood House on The Ridge. He spent his last two years there. He had quietened down somewhat, was less inclined to impose himself, less inclined to dominate and he was certainly less interested in magic. Nevertheless, it is said that on occasion he had fellow lodgers crawling along the floor on all-fours, imagining themselves to be dogs, barking, whining and scratching at the floor. But if that is true it does seem mightily like a party trick compared to those other activities of his earlier years. Was it one asks real magic? Or was this a super hypnotist at work? Most likely a bit of both. Crowley might be best described as part-charlatan and part-genuine black magician of the most awesome kind and most wholly wicked.

Perhaps in these last days at Netherwood House he was keeping in trim his occult skills, his capacity to lead men and women to new universes of terror and the most monstrous visions of foulness. He continued also with his enormous daily doses of drugs, right to the end injecting himself in the armpit with heroin. It is rumoured, incidentally, that after Crowley's death Netherwood House was so terribly haunted that within a year five families who had taken up residence were obliged to move out.

Crowley's cremation service at Brighton Crematorium included his notorious *Hymn to Pan* and caused some outrage among councillors and the more staid members of the community. But what did it matter? Aleister Crowley, the best known practitioner of Black Magic of his time, was gone, no longer caring about this world, no doubt seeking some new place where with his undiminished capacity for wickedness he could continue to cause havoc and terror.

THE CHARMER

------------------------ ❀ ------------------------

L ook at him there, John George Haigh. That quiet smile of his
is like a trademark: he is rarely without it. You can be assured
that he smiled for Mrs Durand-Deacon and for the McSwan

John George Haigh. (Syndication International)

family and the Hendersons. That charmer's smile was there even
when he told the police officers exactly what he had done to his
victims and where and how. And he was still smiling when Mr
Justice Travers Humphreys passed the death sentence on him in
the little pitchpine-panelled courtroom at Lewes. And on the
scaffold at nine o'clock in Wandsworth on 10th August 1949 he
met Albert Pierrepoint with a smile on his face.

All photographs of him show a lightly built, 39 year old man,
one who cares about his appearance. Well-cut suit, shirt collar
sitting nicely, smart tie. And his hair, always neatly barbered and
the moustache trimmed precisely. Even in prison the barber
attends to him on a regular basis. Knowing that he is to hang, he
arranges for Madame Tussaud's to have his lovat-green suit. And
mind, he tells them, do ensure that when the model is exhibited in
the Chamber of Horrors, the shirt cuffs show at least one inch
below the jacket sleeves. And don't forget the trousers: their
creases must be sharp. And the shoes must shine. As they had
done in life.

And that is why John George Haigh fitted in so well at the
Onslow Court Hotel in elegant Queen's Gate, Kensington, where
standards were high in matters of dress. And in other ways too.
And the ladies living there – the residents were for the most part
elderly ladies – liked the reassurance of a man with impeccable
manners, a man well-spoken, an educated man who suited the
genteel atmosphere. Most of his fellow guests appreciated his
quiet charm. And naturally, since he was a long-standing guest,
having been at the hotel since 1944, they trusted him. They lived
with him, these quietly spoken middle-class ladies, never
suspecting for one moment that their Mr Haigh had served three
prison sentences and worse, that since 1944 he had committed
five murders – he would claim eight – and that in his last days in
their company he was to murder one more, one of their own.

So in the dining-room and in the lounge he chats with Mrs
Olive Durand-Deacon, considers her idea. Mrs Durand-Deacon
knows Mr Haigh well for she has been in residence for the past six
years. And like many who met him, the former colonel's wife
found him most interesting. He was an engineer and an inventor.
And of course that was why she had dared to put the notion to

him. Did it sound silly? She had the idea that women might like the idea of artificial fingernails. They could be made of plastic, she thought, and perhaps painted different shades of red and pink and even natural. It had never been tried before but she thought it might catch on. And Haigh agreed. There might be something in it, he told her in his purring tones, his Yorkshire vowels long eroded. Maybe she would like to come down to his experimental laboratory in Crawley. Did she fancy a trip to check out the possibilities? And she did. They arranged to go in a few days' time, on the next Friday. That would be 18th February 1949. So, as arranged, off they went to Crawley. And that was the last anyone ever saw of Mrs Olive Durand-Deacon.

There was some consternation the following morning at the Onslow Court Hotel when Mrs Durand-Deacon did not turn up for breakfast. Nor had her bed been slept in. Mrs Constance Lane, another of the residents, was concerned. What could have happened? She sought out Haigh. Hadn't he intended to take Mrs Durand-Deacon to his workshop the previous day, she asked. Could he shed some light on the matter?

But Haigh was unable to help. Yes, he had intended to take her down to Crawley. They had arranged to meet at the Army and Navy Stores in Victoria at two o'clock. He had gone there to pick her up, he said, but she had not turned up. After hanging about for an hour or so he had left. He was wondering, he now told Mrs Lane, if she had been taken ill or if she had lost her memory. Concerned as Mrs Lane was and worried as Haigh appeared to be, they decided to leave matters as they were. There was sure to be some perfectly sound explanation.

But the next day produced no Mrs Durand-Deacon. Old and frail though she was, Mrs Lane was now determined to go to the police. Haigh said that he would go with her, take her in the Alvis. Doubtless as he walked into Chelsea Police Station he looked as one might expect a successful businessman ought to look in his smart camel overcoat and chamois leather gloves. He and Mrs Lane expressed to the desk sergeant their amazement at their fellow guest's disappearance. Haigh explained about the scheme to manufacture artificial fingernails and about how he had arranged to meet Mrs Durand-Deacon at the Army and Navy

Stores. He described her clothing when last he saw her, leaving the hotel at one o'clock or so. She had been wearing a black hat, a Persian lamb coat and she was carrying a red plastic handbag. But neither he nor Mrs Lane could offer any explanation of what had happened.

At this stage it was simply a missing person case, nothing about it to excite the police. It was, however, the beginning of one of this country's most astounding murder cases.

On Monday 21st February, Policewoman Sergeant Alexandra Lambourne called at Onslow Court, just to fill in any gaps. She spoke to Mrs Lane and to the manager. Then she met Haigh who could add nothing to what he had already said when he and Mrs Lane went to the police station. But whether from intuition or perhaps experience, Alexandra Lambourne was uneasy about Haigh, certain that he knew what had happened to the missing woman. In her report to Detective Inspector Shelley Symes later that day she wrote, 'Apart from the fact that I do not like the man Haigh, with his mannerisms, I have a sense that he is "wrong" and there may be a case behind the whole business.' They must dig further was her suggestion to her senior officer.

And instant queries to Criminal Records produced the information that Haigh had been to jail three times – in 1934, 1937 and 1940 – on each occasion for a series of well-planned frauds.

Sergeant Lambourne's unease about Haigh now seemed well-founded. Inspector Symes thought it might be worthwhile asking help from the West Sussex police. But it was not until the next day, 22nd February, that they were able to clarify matters. Haigh had told them about his links with a small engineering firm, Hurstlea Products, in Crawley. Discussions with Edward Jones, the managing director, revealed the fact that Haigh was a business associate who brought them work and who also placed orders with them from time to time. At Symes' request Sergeant Pat Heslin of Horsham CID and another officer searched the Hurstlea premises but this revealed nothing of any significance.

Then came further useful information from Crawley. An employee at The George Hotel had seen Haigh with a woman at the hotel between four and five o'clock on 18th February. Haigh was well enough known at the hotel. He had been there for the New Year celebrations only weeks earlier. And he had been seen in a restaurant, Ye Olde Ancient Priors, in the early evening.

On 26th February Detective Sergeant Heslin went to see Edward Jones again and for the first time mention was made of a store room in Giles Yard, rented from Hurstlea by Haigh. Here, Jones told the policeman, Haigh carried out 'experimental work' though he was unable to say precisely what the work was.

Heslin, along with Jones and Sergeant Appleton, the local policeman, then went round to Leopold Road where the store house, a rickety two-storey brick building surrounded by a six foot wooden fence, was situated. As the only key was held by Haigh entry was forced.

Inside the whitewashed store they found paint pots, odd pieces of wood and metal, old rags, tools, benches. Not really surprising perhaps. But also on view were a rubber apron, rubber boots, a gas mask, a pair of rubber gloves and a riding mac. There was a stirrup pump, alongside two large carboys and several large oil drums. And what seemed especially out of place was a small leather hat box and a leather briefcase. Both of these contained documents referring to people called McSwan. Nowhere among these documents were there any bearing Haigh's name. And there was a receipt, dated 19th February, from a cleaner in Reigate, for a Persian lamb coat. And in the hat box, with all the papers, were a .38 Enfield revolver and eight live rounds.

The coat was collected from the cleaner's and identified as Mrs Durand-Deacon's by her sister and by Mrs Lane. There was blood on the collar and it was sent to the police laboratories for further examination.

As a result of wide press publicity, a Horsham jeweller now contacted the police. On 19th February, he said, a man calling himself McClean, had come in with items of jewellery. He had wanted to have them assessed. He had called back twice since and had been paid a total of £100. It was the press publicity, however, that jogged an assistant's memory. She recognised him as a man who had brought in jewellery a year earlier, in February 1948. On that occasion he had signed his name as J.G. Haigh of Onslow Court Hotel.

Haigh, immaculate as ever, was brought to Chelsea police station on 28th February where in a drab, buff-painted room he was confronted by Chief Superintendent Tom Barratt, Detective Inspector Albert Webb and Symes. They told him that Mrs Durand-Deacon's coat and jewellery had been recovered and that a revolver, along with some documents, had been found. Yes, Haigh confessed, the coat did belong to Mrs Durand-Deacon and yes, he had sold her jewellery which had enabled him to repay a loan of £36 to Jones and to reduce his overdraft.

At this point, Barratt and Symes were called from the room. Whether or not this was a strategy is unclear. Despite his composure Haigh must have been in turmoil, knowing there was no way out for him now. Suddenly he spoke to Webb who had been left with him in the interview room. 'It's a long story,' Haigh began. 'It is one of blackmail and I shall have to implicate many others. How do I stand about that?' Webb made no conclusive reply and Haigh came out with the question that indicated how he was already working on his defence. 'Tell me frankly,' he asked Webb, 'what are the chances of anyone being released from Broadmoor?' Again Webb was non-committal but he did caution Haigh.

'I understand all that,' Haigh told him, cheerfully frank. 'I'll tell you the truth about it. Mrs Durand-Deacon no longer exists. She has disappeared completely and no trace of her can ever be found again. I have destroyed her with acid. You will find the sludge that remains at Leopold Road. I did the same with the Hendersons and the McSwans. Every trace has gone. How can you prove murder if there is no body?'

It was then, with Barratt and Symes recalled to the room, that Haigh confessed to the murders of Mrs Durand-Deacon and in addition of three people called McSwan and the two Hendersons.

Haigh described how, shortly after her arrival in the store room, when his victim was looking at some papers, he shot her in the back of the head. And then came yet another startling claim. He had made an incision in her throat, he said, and had filled a cup with her blood. And had drunk it. Only after that had he removed her coat and jewellery. And then, he had placed her body lengthwise, head and shoulders first, into one of the oil drums.

His confession continues: 'I then donned the rest of my equipment for I had found it necessary to protect myself from the acid. I had a rubber mackintosh which I kept specially for this purpose, rubber gloves, a gas mask to protect myself from the acid fumes, a rubber apron and rubber boots.' It is all so particular, so precise, so matter of fact, so cold. Then using the stirrup pump he had filled the oil drum with sulphuric acid.

Haigh had then, with the dissolution of the remains under way, felt the need for some refreshment and had gone to Ye Olde Ancient Priors for egg on toast and tea. Later he had returned to the store room and topped up the acid. It was nine o'clock when he finished for the night and went across to the George for dinner before returning to Onslow Court.

Later in his very detailed statement Haigh was to say that Mrs Durand-Deacon, weighing fifteen stone, was 'a confounded nuisance – far more trouble than any of the others. She simply would not disappear.' Catch the slightly exasperated tone. There is no suggestion that he appreciates the enormity of what he has done. His subsequent visits to Leopold Road were annoying because the woman's body would just not dissolve quickly enough. In addition to Mrs Lane's insistence that they visit the police and several interviews with them along with trips to the jeweller's and the dry cleaner's, he had to keep going back to the store room. Three days after the murder, there was still some fat and bone in the drum and it was not until the following day that he felt that decomposition was far enough advanced to pour the 'sludge' out in the yard.

He must have felt himself in the clear now. After all, no body, no proof of murder. Or so he believed. Wrongly. And even if they did catch him he thought that he would be sent to Broadmoor for five years or ten at the outside.

But that was not all, Haigh told the horrified policemen. In 1944 he had murdered Donald McSwan. At the time Haigh, recently released from prison, had a basement workshop in Gloucester Road, London. McSwan, whom he had known for several years, owned amusement arcades and property. He had come to Haigh's workshop with a pinball table for repair. Haigh said he had hit McSwan on the head with a length of piping. He had drunk the dead man's blood and had then immersed the body in acid. He had eventually flushed the residual fluid down a drain in the basement.

Haigh had gone to see McSwan's parents, explaining to them that in order to escape being called up for military service, Donald had gone into hiding in Scotland. In future Haigh told them their son would not correspond with his parents directly but would send letters via his old friend. They seem to have accepted Haigh's story and for nearly a year they received letters purporting to come from Donald. But perhaps the McSwans began to be suspicious. In any event, they suffered the fate of their son in 1945.

Now, claiming to have power of attorney, Haigh disposed of Donald's pinball machines and his several houses. Similarly, everything his parents owned – furniture, private possessions – was sold. And no-one even reported the disappearance of these three people. They had just gone away and no-one ever suspected that the man with power of attorney was their murderer.

But whatever Haigh made from these murders was spent, often at the bookmakers.

By February 1947 when he met Archie and Rose Henderson, a cultured couple, he a doctor, she a beauty, and both wealthy and given to living it up. Haigh worked his way into their lives, became a good friend, a companion with whom they could discuss matters cultural. The former Wakefield Cathedral choirboy was enthusiastic and knowledgeable about music and during his four-year stay in Dartmoor, this eminently able man had taken great advantage of the library facilities to buff up his knowledge of literature. How the doctor and his wife enjoyed Haigh's companionship. And then they went missing. One day they were spending a holiday in Brighton, staying at the Metropole Hotel. And the next they were gone.

On 12th February 1948, a year after their acquaintance began, Haigh disposed of the Hendersons. He persuaded Archie to come up from Brighton to look at the laboratory. 'I drove him to Crawley,' Haigh said, 'and in the store room at Leopold Road I shot him in the head. I then returned to Brighton and told Rose that Archie had been taken ill very suddenly and needed her. I said I would drive her to him. She accompanied me to the store room at Crawley and there I shot her.'

There was the usual blood drinking and then disposal by acid. Relatives and friends received letters with no internal address giving the surprising news that the Hendersons had decided to emigrate to South Africa. Rose Henderson's brother, Arnold Berlin, visited the Hendersons' flat several months after their disappearance and discovered that Rose's jewellery valued at £1,500 and a fur coat worth £400 were missing. Berlin instituted his own enquiries, interviewing 250 people including their friend John Haigh.

So many friends were puzzled by the suddenness of the departure and surprised that there had been no further contact from people who were such sociable animals. But few suspected that they might have been murdered.

In the meantime Haigh sold the Hendersons' car and forged deeds to their house which he then sold. From these transactions he made about £7,700. Most of this went to bookmakers.

This then was the substance of Haigh's confession. A day or so later, he was to say that three others had met similar fates but he could not put names to these. They included a Hammersmith woman; a youth in Kensington; and a girl called Mary whom he met outside the Mansion Hotel on the seafront at Eastbourne. He could not remember if she was there on holiday or working in the town. They had gone first to Hastings and had dinner. Then, he said, 'the urge possessed me'. They drove to Crawley and went to Leopold Road ...

Haigh was not immediately charged with murder. For what if he changed his mind later? It was imperative that the case was made watertight. Or as watertight as possible when there was no corpse. It was essential to establish beyond doubt that Mrs Durand-Deacon had been murdered by Haigh.

Professor Keith Simpson, the Home Office pathologist, inspected the site on 1st March. Inside the building there were splashes of blood on the inside wall. These belonged to Mrs Durand-Deacon's blood group. Inside one of the oil drums were fragments of bone, grease and a hair pin. A bucket and a wooden rod, used presumably for stirring, both had a film of fat.

Simpson had the top three inches of soil over some 47 yards scraped off and packed in five wooden boxes for more detailed examination, which ultimately yielded 28 pounds of yellow fat, spinal discs and traces of pelvic bone. Of most importance were dentures, upper and lower, made of plastic which had not been affected by the sulphuric acid. Mrs Durand-Deacon's dentist was to identify them. The red plastic handbag too had not been consumed and this was found, carelessly hidden in the yard.

On 2nd March 1949, John George Haigh was charged with the murder of Mrs Olive Durand-Deacon.

It was one of the cases of the century. It was such a story that the editor of the *Daily Mirror* was sent to prison for three months for publishing lurid details – 'Vampire Horror in London, SW7' and 'Vampire – A Man Held' ran the headlines – before the case came to court.

The two day trial began on 18th July and the case was heard by the foremost criminal judge of his day, 82 year old Mr Justice Travers Humphreys. And throughout the hearing Haigh sat in the dock, immaculate in a single-breasted fawn suit, his trouser creases as sharp as ever. He was the essence of nonchalance, concentrating not on the proceedings but upon his *Daily Telegraph* crossword.

On the second day, the jury retired to consider the verdict. They were out for fifteen minutes. They agreed with the prosecution argument that Haigh knew what he was doing was against the law and that he knew that what he was doing was punishable. Guilty. And as they took him down and as they drove him away, he still had that rather mild smile on his face.

Bad then? Or mad? On that the jury is still out. Dr Henry Yellowlees, a prominent Harley Street psychiatrist for the defence, stated that Haigh had a 'paranoid constitution', that in medical terms he was a lunatic. But he had to concede that at the same time Haigh was aware of the wrongness of his actions.

But what of the horrifying dreams, always associated with blood, which had plagued Haigh all his life? There had always been in the Haigh household an emphasis on Old Testament blood and horror. He described one such dream. 'I saw before me a forest of crucifixes which gradually turned into trees. At first there appeared to be dew, or rain, dripping from the branches but as I approached I realised it was blood. Suddenly the whole forest

began to writhe, and the trees, stark and erect, to ooze blood …
The blood came from the branches like … A man went to each
tree catching the blood. When the cup was full he approached me
… Drink, he said …'

Those dreams, it has been suggested, were a consequence of an
over-restrictive upbringing by his Plymouth Brethren parents, who
regarded themselves as the 'elect of God', and the contrasting
experience of the exotic High Church ritual of Wakefield
Cathedral where he was a choirboy. Perhaps the conflicts and
tensions were too great for the impressionable adolescent.

After he had killed Donald McSwan, so he said, he dreamed
again of the forest and the blood. Or perhaps he had just realised
that the last pieces of Donald's body were going to be difficult to
get rid of and that he had better finish off the task with a cleaver
and a mincer.

Gruesome? Of course. But did he, as he claimed, live in a
gruesome half world of such horrifying nightmare visions, a world
in which he claimed to be guided by an outside force? Did he
really drink his victims' blood? Was Haigh, under that apparently
calm exterior, absolutely, unequivocally, as mad as it is possible to
be? Or sane? Was he putting it on? Was it all for gain? Or
pleasure?

What does intrigue the follower of Haigh's fortunes is that in
the death cell he showed no fear. His letters to parents and to the
many friends who had been charmed by him never complain
about his present situation. In one letter to his parents he seems
more concerned about the prison laundry service losing a pair of
his socks. He prattles on, in his very fluent fashion, about Sir John
Barbirolli's knighthood, about gardens, about books. He is
besotted with Princess Margaret and her affairs and there are
several references to her. There are many Biblical references too.
And his beautiful regular handwriting refers to the kindness of
friends, so many of whom were devastated to learn what he had
done. To the prison doctor he demonstrates his needle-threading
invention and perhaps the electric toy car and his latest idea for
preventing gas leaks. If you were not to know this man's history,
you might think him a most agreeable man. Yet callous and
pitiless, he never expressed remorse for his deeds. Why should he?

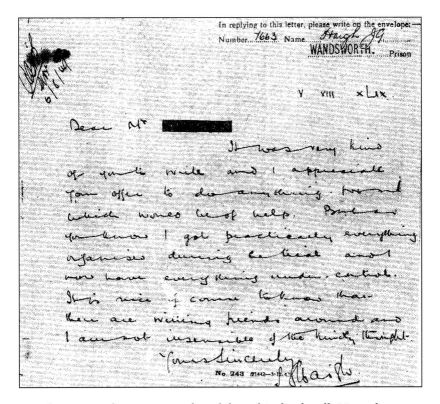

Haigh's postcard written to a friend from his death cell. Note the courteous manner and the meticulous handwriting

Did he not in those last days write, 'We cannot change the inscrutable predictions of the Eternal ... I, that is my spirit, shall remain earthbound for some time: My mission is not yet fulfilled ...'

His mission?

And unperturbed, and apparently agreeably, he presented himself on that last morning to Mr Pierrepoint.

HIDE AND SEEK

——————— ❀ ———————

Beachy Head on a raw December day, 500 feet of sheer white cliff down to the tumbling waves. And further back on the wind-racked grass an abandoned car, a Rover 280. No sign of the driver. Another 'jumper', the police and coastguard concluded. A major land, air and sea search began.

At least they knew who it was they were looking for. Fiona Mont was a well-connected local woman. But one who was in some trouble. In fact she was out on bail. Some scam she'd allegedly been involved in, something to do with computers, selling them and not paying the bills. Perhaps it had all proved to be too much for her. The search for the body lasted two days.

So what had this former public schoolgirl been up to? For the most part nothing greatly different from what she had been up to for much of her life. And yet, far more might have been expected from a woman with such advantages.

Fiona Mont comes from a prominent Lewes family, the youngest of three daughters. Her father was a solicitor and a former Under Sheriff of Sussex, and her mother a former Tory leader of the East Sussex County Council. She had attended St Mary's Hall at Brighton where the fees were £7,000 a year and it was here – though clearly it was no fault of the school – that trouble began. If she was not totally beyond control on school premises, staff were concerned that out of school she was misbehaving seriously. There were suggestions that at week-ends she went out to pubs, drinking excessively. When she was fifteen she was expelled and transferred to Lewes Priory Upper School where her parents believed she would come to her senses and learn to behave. But they were to be disappointed. After only two terms Fiona was suspended because of her unruly behaviour. What

Fiona Mont. (John Connor Press Associates)

could be done with the girl? Her desperate parents took the action that parents with uncontrollable offspring have taken down the centuries. In the 1990s Fiona was dismissed to relatives in Canada for a year.

Her stay in Canada seemed to have done her some good. When she returned to Sussex Fiona appeared to be more mature, more responsible. She found a job as manager of Gemini Business Centre in Brighton. Her family must have breathed a collective sigh of relief. But if they did, there was soon to be a sharp intake of breath. It was the friends she took up with. Just as had always been the case. In her parents' eyes she had always tended to take up with dubious characters. And in Brighton she met Tyrone Bishop, a young sales rep with eleven convictions for car theft. To her he was a compelling figure despite his obvious capacity for being caught in the act. And Tyrone had such lively friends, many of them petty criminals. Just the kind of people that Fiona found so fascinating.

How much more exciting these people were; how much more interesting than the dull, boring people that her parents liked her to mix with. Not that she ever really got into serious trouble with them. Was it because she could talk her way out of anything? Was it that when the police questioned her she ran rings round them. Tyrone Bishop used to laugh at how she had such charm and quickness of thought. 'The Cat', Bishop called her. A cat had nine lives, he used to say. Just like Fiona.

Bishop had ambitions and decided to learn to fly. It would be useful to him as a drug-runner. And he chose just the right kind of flying school when he joined the Baron Flying Club at Shoreham. Here, his instructor was Graham 'The Baron' Hesketh who, in the eyes of Fiona Mont, turned out to be an even more romantic figure than Bishop. He had served a sentence for cannabis smuggling and the possession of a sub-machine gun. Hesketh was in an altogether different league from Tyrone Bishop. Now life was becoming really thrilling.

In December 1999 Fiona Mont was arrested at her basement flat in Sackville Road, Hove, in connection with a £300,000 fraud enquiry. The police claimed that she was responsible for tricking suppliers into forwarding computers and office equipment to various bogus companies in Sussex. But no bills were ever paid. The purchasers vanished and so did the computers. It was a typical 'long firm' scam.

Fiona Mont was questioned at Steyning police station and released on bail. She seemed little disturbed by the charges. While she was still waiting to be charged, one of the officers involved in the case, DC Steve Skerrett, had a phone call from her. Would he

like to call round for a glass of wine? Wisely he resisted. He had
met her at her home on an earlier occasion and was aware of her
ability to charm men. He says, 'She tends to target men to get
what she wants. I spoke to her once and found her in just a bikini.'
And a friend described her as being 'pretty good at manipulating
men. That has been a feature of her life. She was twisting men
around her little finger like she was looking for the one who gave
her the biggest buzz.'

But now for the first time she appeared to be less certain of
herself. She was picked out at an identity parade. And shortly
after that her abandoned car was found at Beachy Head.

Then, after two days searching for the body, the police received
a call from the missing woman's mother. Fiona had telephoned to
say that she was safe. The search for the suicide was called off but
now there was a renewed search for the bail-skipper. A
nationwide hunt was initiated and calls flooded in. There were
reported sightings from County Durham, Dorset, Lancashire and
more close to home from Ardingly and Brighton where she was
said to have been spotted entering a pub. But she was nowhere to
be found. She had simply disappeared. And she was never going
to be easy to find. Police were aware that she was capable of
changing her appearance and assuming new identities. She had
already been known as Frances Montgomery, Alison Miller,
Jacqueline Mayhew, Jemima Chadwick.

Next came information that she was last seen flying out of
Shoreham in a light aircraft, piloted by Graham Hesketh. It was
thought that they had flown to Holland.

In August 2000 Fiona was believed, probably incorrectly, to
have returned to Britain and she was featured on a London
Weekend Television programme, *Britain's Most Wanted*. Hesketh,
however, despite allegedly flying her out of the country, was not
mentioned and apparently was not wanted for any offence.

That same summer Fiona sent e-mails to a national daily,
offering to sell her story. She defied the police, saying that she
would never give herself up. The police, she insisted, were
persecuting her. She was innocent of the fraud charges, she said. If
they wanted her they would have to apprehend her, charge her
and prove her guilty.

Even when on the run, even when pleading her innocence, she constantly teased Skerrett and his colleague DC Dave West, sending them provocative e-mails and faxes. West received a fax addressed to 'The Dave West Fan Club'. On another occasion he received a cheque for £1 million at 'Shoreham Cop Shop'.

Then Skerrett received reports that Fiona had been spotted in Emmelorde in Holland. He contacted Dutch police but they were unable to attend to the matter immediately. When they arrived to arrest the fugitive she had gone.

Fiona next surfaced in November 2001 when she and Hesketh set up a web-site (the-baron.50megs.com) in which she sneered at Sussex police and in particular Skerrett and West, at their inability to catch her, at their persistent unfair hounding of her. The site included references to her TV fame – LWT and now BBC *Crimewatch*. She described herself as '30-year-old Brunette Beauty Fiona Mont', 'Britain's Most Wanted Woman'. It certainly is a self-congratulatory effusion.

'Again and again the national newspapers ran features about this woman who constantly evaded the long arm of the law,' we are told in bold headlines. 'Even the famous INTERPOL were made to look foolish as she gave them the slip too.'

There are also extracts from a book purporting to tell her story, a glamorous tale of devil-may-care outlaws in love. They are romantic, dashing; they are Bonnie and Clyde without the bloodshed. It is not her fault, the synopsis says. She has been falsely accused.

'Fiona's twisted and estranged ex-boyfriend hatched a plot which if it had succeeded would have left her homeless, bankrupt and behind bars. As this true story unravels the reader is sucked into a world of crime, police corruption and intimidation, smuggling, daring aviation escapades, hilarious roller coaster comedy, betrayal, passion, love, jealousy, revenge and criminal genius, initially set in the quiet suburbs of Shoreham-by-Sea' … and so on.

And who is this 'twisted and estranged ex-boyfriend'? Is Tyrone Bishop, who more recently has served a sentence in a French jail for drug smuggling, the author of her woes? Or is it yet another of her ill-chosen friends?

In January 2002, following a tip-off to the *Daily Mail*, Fiona was arrested by Interpol on a caravan site near Malaga. She was living there with Hesketh and their 10 month old daughter Samantha. Present at the arrest was Steve Skerrett who must have felt a great surge of pride and relief that his long pursuit of Fiona Mont was over.

Days later the investigating magistrate in Torremolinos sent her to Madrid to face extradition charges. Hesketh told reporters, 'She will fight extradition. She has not given up.'

Legal process in Spain is sometimes slow. In consequence the Madrid authorities released Fiona on bail. In October 2002, she failed to turn up at the much delayed extradition hearing. She was thought to have fled to Portugal. At the time of writing she is still free and Steve Skerrett and Dave West, who have put in years on this case, fume. But they are patient men. With Fiona Mont they have to be. Ultimately, it is likely that the thrill of being constantly on the run will fade. One of her friends has said that she enjoyed the thrill of crime. But those days, those activities, are surely over. Perhaps she may acknowledge that bringing up a child in such feckless circumstances has to end, that the game is up.

Back at Sackville Road the final demands and the letters threatening legal action continue to drop through the letter box but the present occupant, who found Fiona perfectly charming when he purchased the flat from her days before she disappeared, simply ignores them.

THE DURRINGTON BANK ROBBERY

———— ❊ ————

They were really on their way now. The plan they had talked over and had finalised in the Crown pub in Chiswick in the last seven days was in operation.

Alan was driving, just like in the films, driving through the sheeting rain and the gusting winds and knowing, just knowing, he'd been picked specially for the job by Vic. £200 just for a driving job. Whenever Alan mentioned Vic to his father, he'd be furious. Said he was 'a terrible frightening influence'. Typical of his father to say that, him with his fancy Sales Director's job. Typical of his mother too. They'd been so upset at him going about with Vic that they'd actually moved from Chiswick to Hounslow. But that couldn't separate Alan and Vic. And when Vic said he needed a driver, well, there he was.

And Vic was on a high now. He'd got the shotgun out of the bag and had taken a pop out of the car window, firing up into the night sky. Old Vic, he'd planned it all. He'd sorted out the job. He'd worked in Worthing at the end of the summer and he'd kept his eyes open. And his ears. Then he'd put it all together. Then they'd bought the gun. That would frighten them, Vic had said, when he walked in with a shotgun. That'd put the wind up them.

And there was Philip Tucker, sitting in the back of the Wolseley that they had stolen in Hounslow only hours earlier. Vic had said it looked just like a police car and that would be helpful if they were chased. Of course there had been no key in the ignition and they'd had to break into a garage to get one. Piece of cake, really. And the job would be exciting enough, easy enough, Philip knew that. Vic had sorted that out. But were there no qualms? Did he not wonder, as they sped along the dark after-midnight roads, what his parents were going to say when they found the note?

'I have gone off with Alan,' the 16 year old had written. 'We are going to work around. I'll see you from time to time. Philip.' Only months earlier he'd started as a bank clerk and his mum and dad had been proud of him. But banks were boring. At least being a bank clerk was. But bank robbing, well, that was an entirely

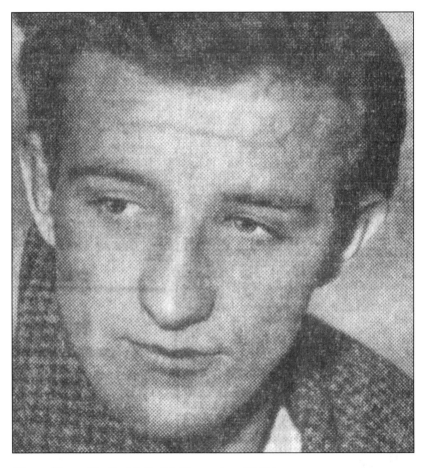

Victor Terry. (Daily Mail, 8th December 1960)

different matter. And this was going to be quite easy, he was sure. There were only two old fellers in the bank, Vic had said.

About two o'clock in the morning they pulled up in a country lane, a dozen miles or so north of Worthing. No point trying to park in the town in the early hours. They would only draw attention to themselves.

But what a night. The wind howled and the rain lashed down. They were cold and uncomfortable. If it hadn't been one of those foul November storms they might have got out of the car, walked around for a while, just to get the blood circulating, just to get more comfortable, just to break the monotony. It wasn't until after 7.30 am, still dark, the rain still lashing down, that they were on the move again, making for Worthing.

They drove to Western Row, just off the seafront, and piled out of the car. Vic knocked at one of the doors. Mrs Salter answered and saw the three boys, bleary-eyed, pasty, their overcoats rumpled. They looked as if they had been sleeping rough, she was to say later. They were strangers until Vic explained who he was. He was Valerie's boyfriend. She was still in bed, Mrs Salter told them, but she asked them to come in. They looked as if they could do with a cup of hot tea.

Mrs Salter knew all about Vic, of course. She'd never met him but she knew he'd been working in the town in the summer and that Valerie was very fond of him. In fact her daughter had spent a couple of week-ends at Vic's home up in Chiswick.

Then Valerie came downstairs, her hair done, her make-up perfect. Did she have to go to work today, she asked her mother. Work was at the little factory where she and her mother were both employed, fitting handles to carrier bags. Couldn't she just stay off, she asked. Just to see Vic for a few hours. So it was that Mrs Salter left the four young people, smoking, drinking tea and listening to the radio.

At 9.40 it was time for the off. It would be all over in an hour, Vic told Valerie. The three boys drove away in their bottle green Wolseley along the seafront and then cut off north to Durrington, only a couple of miles away.

This sub-branch of Lloyd's bank, opened only weeks earlier, in a newly developing area, was on Field Place Parade. The gang was

Victor Terry's girlfriend, Valerie Joan Salter. (News of the World,
11th December 1960)

a shade early. The bank didn't open till ten o'clock. So they parked
for a while in a road behind the shops.

At 10.02 am the car was driven to the front of the bank. Philip
and Vic left Alan behind the wheel, the engine running. They
weren't going to hang around. That's not how bank jobs are done.

Get in, get the money, get out. And there'd be no resistance. Not when they saw the gun, for the moment concealed under Vic's overcoat.

Inside there was only one woman customer. On a day like this, with the skies lowering and the rain sheeting down, there wouldn't be many early birds. Behind the counter there was only one man. A young chap as it happened. The boys had expected somebody old but there was no time to stop to think about that.

Andrew Barker looked up. He was relief cashier today. He'd been called in because of the usual man's illness. Were they expecting builders, he asked himself. These two young men, walking in quite casually, perhaps they were going to do some repairs. And then one of them, the older one, walked down the passageway towards the cloakroom. 'What's this?' the cashier asked. He saw John Pull, the cleaner-cum-guard, coming out of the cloakroom into the passage with the kettle in his hand. First things first. Cup of tea to start the day off. Especially a day like this. And the boy and the cleaner looked at each other.

It was over in moments. A short-barrelled shotgun came out from under the boy's overcoat. Barker later recalled, 'Mr Pull looked completely taken by surprise. For some seconds both myself and Mr Pull just stared. Mr Pull raised his arm, which was a mannerism he had got. He always raised his arm before speaking. He touched the man with the gun on the arm with his hand, but the man with the gun drew away from him slightly and fired.'

At 10.03 am on 10th November 1960, John Pull, 61 years old, family man, retired postman, now a bank employee, President of Worthing Archaeological Society and a major authority on the Stone Age, fell dying with a gunshot wound to the head and a kettle in his hand.

'Where's the money?' Vic asked, turning to the cashier. It was on the counter. It was in a bag which Barker had taken from the vault less than a minute earlier. Philip grabbed it and the two robbers ran out.

Shaken, the cashier set off the alarm and then sought help from neighbouring shopkeepers. Not that there was anything they could do to save John Pull's life. Barker also dialled 999, telling police about the shooting, about the two young men, the car which he mistakenly described as a green MG Magnette. It was all over in less than a minute, he told them.

The boys had dashed out of the bank, Philip first and Vic after him, and had scrambled into the back of the car, Vic shouting at Alan, 'Off you go.' But Alan seemed petrified. He had heard a bang from inside the bank and he only hoped that nothing terrible had happened because he wasn't wanting to be involved in violence, in shooting or anything like that. Vic had said the shotgun was just to put the wind up anybody who didn't do as he was told.

'Have you shot someone?' Alan shouted over his shoulder as he drove off.

'We struggled,' Vic told him.

What did that mean? Alan, anxious, alarmed, took the wrong turning off the roundabout. He couldn't remember the way back to Valerie's house. Had Vic shot and killed somebody? He couldn't concentrate on his driving. And Vic was too busy with the money, transferring it from the bag to an airline hold-all. Vic was the one who knew the way. He knew Worthing. Why didn't Vic say which way to go? He knew the plan. Go back to Valerie's, pick her up and then make for Portsmouth. But Alan couldn't even find his way to Western Row let alone Portsmouth.

This wouldn't do, Vic decided. They'd abandon the car. They left it near the railway crossing in Becket Road. Philip was given the hold-all and he caught a No 4 bus to Worthing railway station. Vic stayed with Alan and they took a No 5 bus to the same destination.

Philip's bus took a longer route and so Vic and Alan decided not to hang around the station. That might be too dangerous. The police would already be on the look-out for them. They might not yet have a detailed description but any two young men hanging around the railway station would be likely to be picked up. So they took a taxi to Valerie's house, thoughtlessly paying an extravagant tip which, had the taxi driver known of the robbery, might well have aroused his suspicions.

They were back at Valerie's house by 10.30 am but then Vic sent Alan back to the station to pick up Philip. When Alan found him the youngster had been busy. He had gone into a lavatory cubicle and had transferred the money from the hold-all to his pockets. The hold-all he had stuffed behind a lavatory pedestal. Then another taxi ride to Valerie's house; another excessive tip.

At Western Row Philip emptied his pockets of over £1,000 and Vic handed bundles of notes to the two boys. When they met at Portsmouth later, he told them, he would share it out fairly. Valerie said later that Vic gave her some money to hide and she refused to touch it. But when he tried to hide bundles of notes behind a picture frame, she took them from him and carried them upstairs. She hid the money in a handbag in the wardrobe. The robbers' overcoats were also hidden in the wardrobe.

The next stage of the plan was to get out of Worthing. Vic and Valerie would stay together and Alan and Philip would pair up. They would all meet up at Portsmouth Harbour later.

Alan and Philip were the first to leave the house. They went to the promenade and waited for a bus. Within minutes police, on the look-out for two young suspects, spotted them, two boys on a miserable winter's day, standing at a bus stop wearing only sweaters and jeans. They'd just come down from London, they said. They'd packed up their jobs and were off to Cornwall on holiday. Going to Cornwall on holiday? In November? And with no luggage?

And as Vic and Valerie, who had left the house not three minutes later, passed by on the Littlehampton-bound bus, they saw the policemen questioning the others at the bus-stop, asking about the £60 found in Philip's pockets and the £100 roll of £5 notes in Alan's possession.

At Littlehampton Vic and Valerie stopped to consider the next step, feeding the juke box with coins in the café where they had lunch. They decided to take a taxi to Portsmouth.

Perhaps it is time to consider briefly Valerie Salter's part in all this. For it does sound grossly callous of her to be listening to pop music with so light a spirit when an old man has just been shot by her lover. But she was eighteen. She was deeply in love. She knew that Vic had robbed a bank even though his arrival in Worthing only hours earlier had surprised her. He had told her some time earlier that that was what he planned to do. She had tried to dissuade him for she had never been in any kind of trouble. But he'd made up his mind. And maybe somewhere in her mind was the idea that at least this robbing and running was life, was better than that boring old factory. Perhaps the romantic notion of being on the run with the man she loved took hold of her.

So now, Valerie willingly followed Vic's lead. They caught a taxi to Portsmouth. By this time, of course, there were alerts throughout Sussex and the neighbouring counties. Road blocks were set up on all major roads, the police on the look-out for two young men in a green MG Magnette.

The first road block was just outside Littlehampton where the constable glanced quickly at the couple in the back of the taxi and waved them on. They passed equally easily through the second road block at Barnham, nine miles further along the road. At the Chichester by-pass road block a sergeant explained that a bank guard had been shot dead and this seems to be the first time that Valerie heard of the shooting. 'Oh, they shot and killed him,' Vic said. 'I wonder who did it.' He told the policeman that his name was Weston and that he lived in Littlehampton. Valerie said that she was Valerie Brown, also from Littlehampton. They said that they were going to Portsmouth on a shopping spree. They were marrying shortly, they said.

The taxi driver entertained no doubts about his passengers. Typical young couple in love was his assessment. He finally dropped them at Portsmouth Harbour where Vic told him he was meeting friends. But the others did not turn up. Vic guessed what had happened.

The couple stayed the night at a Southsea guest house, passing themselves off as honeymooners, 'Mr and Mrs Diamond of Greenford, Middlesex.'

Back in Worthing the police had discovered from Alan and Philip the link with the Salters. They called Mrs Salter, an eminently respectable woman, from the factory and searched the house. In the wardrobe they found the money in the handbag and the overcoats, one of which was bloodstained. The bolt action of the shotgun was in the pocket of one of the coats. There were also love letters from Vic to Valerie which gave his Chiswick address. As a consequence police kept a watch on his parents' house.

The police now knew who they were looking for. They knew that the young men they had already arrested were Alan Hosier, a 20 year old from Hounslow and 16 year old Philip Tucker from Chiswick. Neither had a criminal record. And the gunman on the run was Victor Terry, also 20 years of age, a young man with a record of violence.

Why on earth was an essentially decent girl like Valerie Salter mixing with the likes of Vic Terry? The despair of caring parents, he'd never stuck at any job. A housebreaker, a mugger, he had twice been sent to Borstal. The first time was for attacking an elderly man for his wallet. The second Borstal spell was after coshing a bank cashier.

Vic, with his velvet collars, his winkle pickers, his drainpipe trousers, mixed with the Chiswick Teddy boy gangs in a world of juke boxes and pin tables, of violence and viciousness. In his head there existed a whole world of gangsterism, a world of fights and shootings, in which he was somebody. 'I'll hang one day,' he bragged. They'd remember him. One day he'd do a really big job. But until his last job, the incompetent bank robbery, he committed only small offences, the kinds of crimes for which he was most fitted.

In the summer of 1960 Vic worked for a week or so in a coffee bar in Eastbourne – he broke into MacFisheries there – before moving on to Worthing where he first worked in Le Panorama Club, a dingy, rather dubious place on the seafront. Then he found work at the Dome as a handyman.

Vic was heavily into drugs at this time which were easily available in the rather sedate town to those in the know. It was Purple Hearts in those days and Benzedrine. He was sacked after five or six weeks when one of the Directors of the Dome found him sitting at a table – 'in gangster-like fashion', he said – with one foot up on the table while a group of adoring girls watched him throwing tablets in the air and catching them in his mouth. Purple Hearts.

At the time the Worthing bank robbery was being planned, only days before it was carried out, Vic was described by one of his friends: 'His cheeks were drawn in while the pupils of his eyes were dilated. He was shaking with nervousness. He couldn't stop talking. His tongue was dry and swollen.' And this was the leader of the gang.

Yet Valerie had not given up on him. She seems not to have seen him as the unstable man he really was. So on from Southsea she went with him. How did either of them expect this to end? Did they really believe they could run and run for ever?

The next day they took a taxi from Southsea to Salisbury where, after lunch, Vic bought another shotgun. This time, because the taxi driver was with them, he called at a post office and bought a gun licence, again using the name 'Diamond'. Then it was London, Euston and the train to Scotland. They must now, registering as 'Mr and Mrs Parker' in a Glasgow guest house, have felt far enough away and safe. But the landlady recognised them from the TV news and alerted the police.

When Detective Inspector Hector Black called on them shortly after midnight on 13th November, Vic assured him that his name was Parker and that he and his wife were on holiday from Manchester. But when the policeman asked to look at the tattoos on his arm – they read 'Maureen', 'Mabel', 'Vic', and 'Knife', all crudely worked by needle and boot polish – he knew he had his man. And had he needed further confirmation there was the gun licence in Vic's pocket in the name of 'Diamond'.

Later that day, under arrest, Vic and Valerie were flown back to London.

In March 1961 the eight-day trial took place at Lewes. Victor Terry, Alan Hosier and Philip Tucker were accused of murder and robbery at Durrington and the theft of £1,372 from the bank. Valerie Salter was charged with receiving £928, knowing it to have been stolen, and with 'sheltering and harbouring Victor Terry while knowing he had murdered John Pull'.

The facts spoke for themselves. The prosecution case was cast-iron. Geoffrey Lawrence QC, for the prosecution, described it as 'a grim and shocking story' especially as it involved four young people. He rejected Vic's claim that Pull had handled the gun and that in the struggle it had gone off. Forensics had proved that only Vic Terry's prints were on the weapon.

The defence suggested that even if there were no prints on the gun the suddenness of the guard's involuntary gesture, raising his hand prior to speaking, might have caused Vic to fire. But the major plank of the defence was that Vic Terry was unstable, that he suffered from diminished responsibility, that he lived in a mental no-man's-land located somewhere between sanity on one side and insanity on the other. There was some insanity in the family, the defence argued. And there were the hallucinations too.

Vic Terry claimed that his body and mind were invaded by the spirit and mind of the American gangster 'Legs' Diamond, who was shot to death in 1931. Diamond was the name he used in the Southsea guest house and on the gun licence. It was an obsession with him, said Alan King-Hamilton for the defence. 'It was not Terry and the girl who were going away. It was 'Legs' Diamond and his gangster's moll.' This was a man who was subject to moods and delusions consistent with schizophrenia, a man urged by voices to be a lawbreaker. His mother told the court that he had spoken to her about the problem. 'The voice had told him that he had got to do these things,' she said.

After eight days the jury rejected the claims of possession and the suggestion that Pull had in some way contributed to the shooting. They found Vic Terry guilty of murder and he was sentenced to death. Alan Hosier and Philip Tucker were found guilty of non-capital murder. Hosier received a life sentence and Tucker was detained during the Queen's pleasure.

Valerie Salter was placed on probation for 12 months. Mr Justice Stable, that most humane of judges, was deeply concerned about her. 'If ever a human being was put in an appalling dilemma, you were. I suppose there is nothing sadder than to see the things we believe in, and perhaps love, shattered ... Go back to your friends and family and start life afresh.'

Before his execution on 25 May 1961, Vic Terry wrote to Valerie. He explained that he did not really love her. And as she would see in the newspaper, another girl was having his baby. We are reminded of how Pinkie, the boy-gangster in *Brighton Rock*, left a similar brutal message for his girlfriend.

Valerie Salter changed her name. The old Valerie was gone, she said. 'In her place, I hope, there's someone who wants to do something decent in life.'

Let's all hope so. And let's hope the same for Alan Hosier and Philip Tucker.

THE ARTIST

———— ✿ ————

Much of John Cockett's life is a mystery. There are great gaps in it. We know that he was born in Uckfield and that he went to Haywards Heath grammar school until 1964, leaving when he was sixteen with six 'O' levels. Then there was a spell with the Atomic Energy Commission at Amersham where he did seem to be a very bright boy. His boss, Dr Catch, was very impressed by him. Young Cockett was promising, could talk a good talk about physics even though it was apparent that he had not mastered the basics. It seemed that he was able to memorise chunks of the textbooks. The best thing he could do, Dr Catch told him, was to take a day-release course and pass the subject at 'A' level. Then there would be a future for him at the AEC. But at the age of nineteen Cockett dropped out of the course. The work was too easy, he said. And then he resigned from the AEC. There was already a disdainful air about him.

In 1970 he comes on the scene again. He has applied for a teaching post at Hazelwick School in Crawley. He has done research at Oxford, he says. The headmaster rubs his hands, delighted to find such a rare gem, a science teacher with a doctorate. Physicists are rare enough to find. Physicists who are so highly qualified are even rarer in comprehensive schools. Just the man he needs for the sixth form. The head knows him as Dr John Drewe. Alas for Hazelwick, in a matter of weeks Cockett – or Drewe as we shall know him in future – is on his way. An old acquaintance has recognised him.

Next port of call was an Orthodox Jewish school in North London. Here staff picked up hints that he had done some secret work for the government. There were suggestions that he had been a spy. Perhaps some might have thought that that was the reason for his leaving the school in somewhat mysterious circumstances. This reference to espionage would be a constant theme and one must wonder if there is not some truth in it. The secret services have as great a share of the seedy, the unreliable, the glib, the oddball and the downright dishonest as any other profession.

But what happens between 1970 and the 1980s when he arrives once more centre-stage? Where was he all these years? What was he doing? Nowhere was there any official record of his holding a steady job or paying tax; there was no record of any criminal convictions. Yet he drove expensive cars, was a qualified helicopter pilot and appeared to be very wealthy. Where did the money come from? At times, he passed himself off as Professor John Drewe, claiming to have links with the Israeli Secret Service, trying to recover a stolen plan for a 'Stealth' helicopter. On other occasions he was a nuclear physicist who had written papers for the Soviet Union about Western technology. A South African secret agent, he has said, has engaged him to sell works of art to raise money for arms. But he is no crank. These tales have been covers for whatever scams he has been engaged in over many years. The dapper John Drewe, articulate, convincing and charming, is one of our most brilliant conmen. And at the same time he might have been involved in espionage. He might ...

It is unlikely that his greatest coup would have been discovered had he not walked out on Bathsheva Goudsmith, the Israeli woman he had lived with for sixteen years. In 1994 there began a long, acrimonious custody battle for their two children and a further civil case in which she sought a share of his assets.

Among the papers Drewe had left at home, Bathsheva found evidence of what she regarded as a further betrayal. 'I was so horrified when I read them that I took them to the police,' she said. Over the years Drewe had brought home scores of paintings, purportedly by famous artists. He had told Bathsheva that they belonged to John Catch, his former AEC boss, who was, he said, now Lord Chelmwood, a peer of the realm. Since his earliest years, Drewe told Bathsheva, Catch had supported him, helped him with his studies, given him money and now intended to leave him all his £2 million fortune. According to Drewe, Catch now wished to sell some family paintings but did not want this to be widely known. He was paying Drewe a handsome commission for each painting he sold.

But the documents Bathsheva found in the house revealed the truth about the paintings. After three years of police investigation, Drewe's trial began in September 1998 and lasted four and a half months. Evidence was given by witnesses from the United Kingdom, the United States, France and Israel. The stories they told revealed an astonishing bravura criminal performance by Drewe and a scarcely believable gullibility on the part of the art world. For ten years Drewe had deceived galleries, art houses, critics, painters, private collectors and a whole host of highly regarded experts. And it had all seemed so simple.

Who would have even thought of such a scam in the first place? There, jammed among the adverts in *Private Eye*, was what most of us would have regarded as a rather eccentric idea. A chap in Staffordshire was offering to paint 'genuine fakes' from £150 a painting. These were not copies of originals: they were paintings in the style of modern artists such as Marc Chagall, Alberto Giacometti, Ben Nicholson, Nicholas de Stael and Graham Sutherland. Bit of fun really to have a painting hanging on your walls from a top-notcher like one of those. There was nothing illegal about it: they were only painted 'in the style of'. And the artist did not even forge the names of the artists he copied. He put his own name on the canvases – John Myatt.

Myatt, a former schoolmaster, made a modest living from this. Not really enough for his needs if truth were known. He was just about getting by. And then John Drewe contacted him, John Drewe, who apparently presented himself as a research scientist employed by the government to inspect nuclear submarines, a man who Myatt was inclined to believe, when he put two and two together, was involved with British intelligence. Impressive.

At first Myatt was under the impression that Drewe wanted the pictures for his own home. But then Drewe made his proposal. Why confess to the public that he was producing 'genuine fakes', he asked Myatt. Why be satisfied with a couple of hundred pounds for his work? Why not announce that these were genuine lost paintings? If Myatt would produce the paintings Drewe

John Myatt, art forger

would find a market for them. There was money in it. And Myatt, fascinated by the man, and perhaps intimidated too, agreed to become Drewe's partner in crime. Of course, he needed the money.

Over the years Myatt created scores of 'lost' works by modern masters. Some of the paintings were very speedily executed. A Ben Nicholson, for example, took no more than two hours to complete. At times he used unorthodox methods and strange materials. To fake a de Stael he mixed household emulsion and KY lubricating jelly in order to imitate the brush strokes in the originals. Contents of the vacuum cleaner bag were sometimes emptied onto the canvases in an attempt to age them. The tacks on the frames were coated with salt in order to rust them. Signatures, copied from books about artists, were forged. Four Le Corbusiers were sold for £110,000. Over the next few years Drewe paid Myatt up to £100,000.

Drewe also helped to age the pictures. Bathsheva recalled seeing him in the garden, putting mud on paintings. In answer to her very proper query, for she believed that these were the legitimate property of John Catch, he said that although they were old, they had been in the vaults for so long they still looked new. Perhaps, he said, people would not believe they were genuine if they looked too new. And she was persuaded.

For his part, Myatt was very surprised that his paintings were accepted without demur. Quite recently he admitted this. 'You know the amount of effort that went into them was ... minimal, quite honestly. Any second or third year art student at college now could do what I did. It was not well researched. I never bothered about the original canvas. I never bothered about textures and touch.'

The truth was that he paid little attention to detail. He used paints developed years after the works were supposedly produced and some of the paintings lacked the essential characteristics of their supposed creators.

So how did Myatt's really quite modest fakes pass the scrutiny of those who ought to have known better? The first essential was that the artists should be dead. There was no artist popping up to disclaim suddenly discovered works. That was important. But it was also important to deceive the dealers and gallery owners, the academics, the directors of major national institutions. And this was where Drewe's genius was required. It was he who provided the appropriate documentation which appeared to verify the authenticity of the paintings when they arrived on the market.

With paintings by major artists it is essential to know their previous history. Perhaps it is not inappropriate to compare this authentication to the log book of a second-hand car. If a particular painting's provenance is acknowledged by august bodies such as the Tate or the National Gallery or the V&A, then there is less likelihood of its being bogus. It was Drewe's skill in concocting convincing provenances for 200 of Myatt's paintings that enabled this majestic fraud to work for ten years.

Drewe used notepaper from the 1940s and 1950s on which he printed letter-heads from galleries. On these, using one of his three old typewriters, he invented descriptions of paintings on which the paint was scarcely dry. There were receipts dating back forty, fifty, sixty years. False catalogues from years past mentioned by name Myatt's latest efforts. There were old file cards, stained and crumpled, giving further details. Half a dozen rubber date stamps – one from the Tate Gallery, another stolen from a firm of solicitors – authenticated the long progress of month-old Myatts. And there were photographs taken on old cameras and these, labelled, dated, were attached to letters and cards. For over ten years, Drewe inserted these details into the archives of the greatest art galleries in the land.

Access to the archives is difficult. Approach the galleries and ask to see the archives and you are likely to be dismissed in short order. Yet Drewe managed to have almost unlimited access to wherever he wished to go. A £20,000 donation to the Tate Gallery eased his entry. Obviously he was to be trusted as a serious researcher. Easy.

At the Victoria and Albert bogus character references describing him as 'an art historian of integrity', paved the way. Simple.

Bill McAlister, the Director of the Institute of Contemporary Arts, enjoyed his lunches in Soho with Drewe whom he found to be a charming man, so knowledgeable about art. And after he donated two paintings which raised £20,000 at an ICA charity auction he was welcomed with open arms. Even though the paintings were fakes. Piece of cake.

From now, with a free run, he doctored the archives, inserting his fake provenances. He photographed old catalogues, removed provenances which contradicted his false histories, inserted his own convincing forgeries. One of his faked receipts showed that one of Myatt's latest paintings, purporting to be a Giacometti, sold for £1,900 in 1958. Now it sold to an American gallery for over £100,000. In this case, to make doubly sure of the painting's authenticity, the gallery called in experts – alas, from a company run by Drewe. Sir Alan Bowness, the Tate Gallery Director in the late 1980s, accepted twenty pictures on the strength of their documentation. A Ben Nicholson realised £107,000 in the United States. The catalogue of an exhibition held years earlier at the defunct Hanover Gallery was replaced by a bogus version itemising some of the fakes. A leading London art dealer bought a fake Sutherland for £5,250. In all, this particular expert, who sometimes appears on the television Antiques Road Show, bought other pieces to the tune of £40,000.

Neither Drewe nor Myatt could approach galleries or auction houses with the 'discoveries' of 'lost' paintings. They needed to detach themselves as much as possible from the enterprise. For his purpose Drewe employed 'runners', each of them equipped with appropriate documentation, to visit Christie's and Sotheby's and like establishments. The 'runners' were given different accounts of the pictures' provenances. One, for example, was told that they were being disposed of by a man who did not wish his children to know he was selling them. Drewe persuaded a former neighbour, Clive Belman, 'a good salesman who knew nothing about art', to act as a 'runner'. He told Belman that he belonged to a syndicate wishing to sell 300 paintings stored in safe deposit boxes. The

Art fraud mastermind is sentenced to six years

By Joanna Bale

A CONMAN who committed the century's biggest contemporary art fraud was jailed for six years yesterday by a judge who told him that he had inflicted immeasurable damage on the art world.

John Drewe, 50, made at

as he was sentenced by Judge Geoffrey Rivlin, QC, who said at Southwark Crown Court that he had been the "chief architect, organiser and driving force behind a massive fraud". He added: "The evidence in this case reveals you

ed on Friday. The judge then turned to Myatt, who admitted conspiracy, telling him that his part in the fraud was so "vital and so significant" it was impossible to accede to defence pleas that his prison sentence be suspended. The

'Genuine fakes' or the real thing?

sales, Belman was told, would fund the purchase of archive material to 'disprove the revisionist theory of the Holocaust'. Belman, who was Jewish, saw it as a worthy cause.

Drewe paid a retainer to Daniel Stoakes, a former schoolfriend and now an impoverished psychiatric nurse in Exeter, to pose as the owner of a collection of Ben Nicholsons. Stoakes was later to say in court that he had not understood that he was part of a conspiracy to defraud and the court accepted his plea of innocence.

At the lengthy trial at Southwark Crown Court which concluded in February 1999, Drewe and Myatt were charged with conspiring to defraud fine art dealers, experts, auctioneers and collectors between 1st January 1986 and 4th April 1996. Myatt pleaded guilty to the charges but gave evidence for the prosecution.

Drewe, having dismissed his counsel on the second day of the trial, defended himself stoutly and persuasively. He maintained that he had been selling genuine pictures and the money was going to Allivane International Ltd, a firm which he said was a front for the Special Intelligence Services who were exporting arms to Iraq and Iran. Now, Drewe claimed, he was the victim of a government conspiracy to keep the matter quiet.

John Bevan QC, prosecuting, said that despite his claims, Drewe's main aim had been to make money. At the same time, he said, this highly intelligent man, contemptuous of experts, had taken an intellectual delight in fooling people.

It was claimed that Drewe made as much as £1.8m from sales of the fakes but that only 70 had been recovered from London, Paris and New York. As many as 140 were still unaccounted for and these might be in private collections or even in the store rooms of some of the embarrassed major galleries.

Drewe was ultimately found guilty of masterminding what was undoubtedly the biggest contemporary art fraud in 20th century Britain. He was to serve three years of a six year sentence. Myatt was sentenced to a year in jail and served four months.

So what about Drewe, that charming and skilful operator? His strategy according to one critic 'was more than just sneaky. It was brilliant.' He has been described as anarchic, hostile to authority, a deluded genius, unrepentant and unscrupulous, a flamboyant Walter Mitty character. He has, in corrupting major art archives, damaged Britain's art heritage. Undoubtedly the work of the artists involved has been devalued.

And then there's John Myatt who could never have believed that a simple advertisement in the columns of *Private Eye* would lead to such an upheaval in his life. On release from prison in 1999 Myatt put on a show in an art gallery in Warwick. There was an unbelievable response; several of his works sold in advance. Since then he has been in demand. 'There are a lot of people out there who can fake pictures,' he says, 'but what people want is a John Myatt fake.'

And where is Drewe now? Born in 1948 he is presumably out and about. And if so, is his inventive genius dormant? Or is it, is he, active? And if so, is it as a conman? Or as a spy?

THE EVIDENCE AGAINST

―――――❖―――――

The Hastings police surgeon, called to the substantial Victorian semi in Lower Park Road, said later that in his long experience he had never before encountered so horrific a crime scene. Blood stained the dining-room floor, the trellis, the newly painted patio doors. The girl lay on the tiled patio in a pool of blood, her skull shattered. By her head was the heavily bloodstained weapon, an 18-inch metal tent peg, the kind used in the erection of marquees. The victim, Billie-Jo Jenkins, was 13 years old.

As the surgeon made his assessment Sion Jenkins was describing to the police what had happened when he and his daughters, Annie and Lottie, had returned home that afternoon. He opened the front door, he said, and the two girls ran in ahead of him. It was 10 year old Lottie who had screamed. 'Dad,' she shouted, 'Billie's hurt'.

Jenkins had gone out to the patio. Billie-Jo was dying, dead. He had placed his arms around the child but what could he do? She looked beyond help. And Annie and Lottie were hysterical. He needed to get them out of the way, needed to calm them, soothe them. Billie-Jo had had an accident, he told them. But she was going to be all right. He ushered the two girls into the playroom and phoned for an ambulance. His foster-child had fallen down, he said. She was hurt. And then he waited what seemed like an eternity for the ambulance to arrive. In the meantime, he telephoned a neighbour, Denise Franklin. Would she come in, he asked. Mrs Franklin, a qualified first-aider, took over but detected no pulse. Meanwhile Jenkins dialled 999 a second time. The ambulance men, when they arrived, attempted resuscitation but it was all too late for Billie-Jo.

Jenkins explained to the police that it had been a Saturday much like any other. At least the weather had picked up after a

Sion Jenkins. (John Connor Press Associates)

week of rain and cold, February at its worst. Today, Saturday, the sun was out, the wind had dropped, the air was mild. Not a bad day for Billie-Jo and Annie to get on with some household chores. The girls were keen to make some extra pocket money. Billie-Jo also had an extra incentive: she had an eye on a pair of Reebok trainers she had seen in Debenhams.

Not that the organisation of the work was simple. The utility room had to be tidied up; the patio doors, damaged some months earlier by an intruder, needed to be painted. But there was a squabble between 12 year old Annie and Billie-Jo. Both wanted to paint the patio doors. Jenkins and his wife Lois, a social worker, mediated. Finally the problem was resolved. Billie-Jo would start on the doors and then, after Annie had finished the utility room, she would move on to the painting. At lunchtime, all details were finalised. Annie would take over the painting of the doors at four o'clock and Billie-Jo would then be free to go to town to buy her trainers.

In the afternoon, Lois took the younger children, 8 year old Esther and Maya, 7, for a walk on the beach. Lottie went off to her two o'clock clarinet lesson. And Billie-Jo and Annie set about their tasks. But Billie-Jo was not being entirely successful and several times Jenkins had to show her how to paint. But it was all good-humoured and at one point, in a playful moment, Billie-Jo jumped on her foster-father's back.

Sometime before three o'clock, Jenkins told the two girls he was going to pick up Lottie from her class. It was such a fine day, he told them, he was going to put the roof down on the MG convertible. Would they like to come with him? 'Yes,' said Annie. 'No,' said Billie-Jo. She wanted to finish the painting.

When Jenkins and Annie arrived to pick up Lottie she had a friend with her. Jenkins told the girl he would give her a lift home. When they arrived at the house in Elphinstone Road, the mother of Lottie's friend noted the time as she had expected her daughter rather earlier and had been anxiously watching the clock.

Jenkins drove his daughters home but, within minutes of entering the house, he told them they would have to go out again. They needed some white spirit, he said. They'd go down to the local Do It All and buy some. Back they all climbed in the car.

But what a roundabout route they took. He would not have gone that way ordinarily. It would have been much quicker had he just turned the car in the road but he had not wanted to make a three-point turn. So now he drove from home down to Bethune Way, where he turned left. He turned left again into St Helen's Road. Suddenly Jenkins changed his mind. They weren't going to Do It All. They were going back home, he said. He turned left into Dordrecht Way and then once more into Lower Park Road. But why, the girls asked. No point in buying white spirit, he told them. It was too late for Annie to start painting today. The paint would never dry. But Annie pleaded, wheedled. Can't I paint today? I want to paint today. The paint will dry. Her father was quite

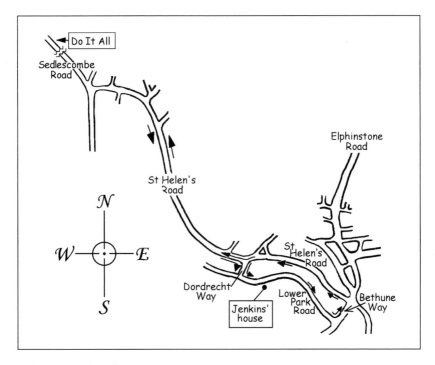

The route taken by Jenkins to the DIY store

quickly persuaded so now he drove past the house, back down to Bethune Way, turned once more, and then made for Do It All in Sedlescombe Road North. It was a slight diversion, wasting perhaps no more than two or three minutes. But when they finally reached the store, he realised that he had forgotten to bring any money. He'd come out without his wallet, he said. They would have to go home.

At the house now for the second time, Jenkins opened the front door and the children ran in front of him. And Lottie shrieked, 'Billie's hurt'. And he went out to the patio …

That is what Sion Jenkins told the police about the events of Saturday 15th February 1997.

And who could disbelieve him? For the 39 year old Sion Jenkins was a pillar of the community, a respected schoolmaster, a regular churchgoer. Since 1992, when he had moved from London, he had been deputy headmaster at William Parker Boys' School in Hastings and was now head-designate of the school which he was to take over on the retirement of the existing headmaster in the summer.

A caring couple, Jenkins and Lois had fostered Billie-Jo for the last five years and had recently started proceedings to adopt her formally. The girl, from a seriously troubled background in the East End, had settled well, was now acknowledged as a much loved sister, and was described variously as 'polite,' 'mature,' 'delightful.'

After the police interview the family left the house to stay with friends. The police took with them the clothing worn by Jenkins and his two daughters. For elimination purposes.

Apparently the police had some suspicions about who might have committed the murder. The house next door to the Jenkins was unoccupied. It was the police view that whoever had murdered Billie-Jo had hidden in the garden of the empty house, watching her painting the patio doors, waiting until Jenkins and Annie left. The newspapers carried stories about prowlers in the area; the *Daily Mirror* mentioned a man with a scarred face; Lois Jenkins mentioned that an intruder had damaged the patio door; Sion Jenkins had had security lights fitted and spoke of having found an intruder in the garden only twelve days earlier.

And on Wednesday 19th February the police sought one particular suspect, a man with a history of mental disturbance, who had been seen in Lower Park Road on the afternoon of the murder. They spoke to his psychiatrist but made no immediate progress with this line of enquiry. The man was later sent to hospital. Later a second man was arrested and released.

Then came the bombshell. On Monday 24th February, the police took Sion Jenkins into custody. After two days he was released on bail but warned that enquiries were continuing. He was ordered not to go near his family. If he did so, his children would be taken into care. The police warned him for his own safety to leave Hastings and he went off to his parents' home in Aberystwyth.

This astonishing police turnabout was a consequence of the findings of the forensic scientists who had identified spots of blood on Jenkins' clothing. Only under a microscopic examination had they become apparent: 72 spots on the fleece jacket, 76 on the trousers and three on the left shoe.

In March Jenkins returned to Hastings to see the children. Like all his subsequent meetings with them, this was organised by the police and attended by Lois and a social worker. But it was on this first occasion that Jenkins was arrested and charged with murder and deception before his children had left the building. Whilst it does suggest that the police were supremely confident that they had the right man, it smacks nevertheless of some insensitivity as far as the children were concerned.

Immediately after this the public were astounded to learn from their newspapers that the respected schoolmaster had lied about his qualifications. He had never been a pupil at Gordonstoun. He had never graduated from the University of Kent. He was again bailed and returned once more to Wales where for 15 months he awaited trial. During this time Lois, his wife for fifteen years, became openly hostile to him, accusing him of beating her.

The trial opened in Lewes on 3rd June 1998, Mr Justice Gage presiding. The prosecution advanced no motive for the murder. Perhaps Jenkins had simply lost his temper with the girl; perhaps he thought her paintwork was sloppy; perhaps he objected to her playing the radio too loudly; perhaps it had something to do with what the prosecution vaguely described as their 'complex relationship' but about which they produced no evidence.

The prosecution was dismissive of the account of the journey to Do It All. The reason why Jenkins had taken the girls off with him to buy white spirit, they argued, was to set up an alibi. Returning to the house after Lottie's clarinet lesson, he had killed Billie-Jo with the tent peg, and then needed to get away from the house in order to give time for an imaginary murderer to enter the house. Hence the protracted trip to Do It All. It was time-wasting, giving him time to think, and time for his 'intruder' to make his entry.

But it was the evidence of the blood on his clothing which told most strongly against Sion Jenkins. A fine spray of blood, a mist of infinitesimal spots, revealed under the microscope, was the final proof that he was a child-killer. The defence argued that the blood had been breathed onto him as he had held the dying girl in his arms. Jenkins himself said in court: 'I noticed a bubble of blood from her nose; I believed she was alive.' Whilst the prosecution accepted that some movement of her body might well have released trapped air, they refused to acknowledge the possibility of its having enough power to project the blood all over his clothing.

It was the blood more than anything else which sent Sion Jenkins to prison for life. It was a unanimous verdict by the jury.

After the trial there was little sympathy for this despicable man, this 'control freak, prone to violent outbursts of temper.' Lois, now absolutely turned against him, sought a divorce. The *Sun* headline screamed, 'Jenkins secretly harboured vile desires for the 13 year old'. The *Guardian* highlighted his 'volcanic temper.' He was a womaniser, a wife- and child-beater.

Jenkins' appeal in December 1999 was unsuccessful. He was the last known person to see Billie-Jo alive and the first to see her dead; the circuitous trip to Do It All was plainly an attempt to establish an alibi, made all the more unconvincing because he already had white spirit in the house and because he had not bothered to take any money with him; and the blood spots were absolutely conclusive. Jenkins was denied the right to appeal to the House of Lords.

So, for the present, Sion Jenkins, found guilty of the murder of a 13 year old child in his care, continues in gaol. It is the right place for him, so many say.

And yet ... and yet, is he really guilty of this appalling crime?

Let's first of all consider his presenting wittingly false details when he was appointed to William Parker Boys' School in 1992. Of this he was undoubtedly guilty. He had a teacher training certificate but without his pretended graduate status he might not have been appointed deputy headmaster. He certainly worked his way up the promotion ladder unfairly. Not that he is a man without ability. At the end of 1992 he was awarded a Master of Science degree in Educational Management by the University of East London. And in the following years his work was so impressive that he was appointed as the next headmaster of William Parker. In October 2002 Roger Mitchell, his headmaster at William Parker for five years, the man Jenkins was intended to succeed, wrote that he still had 'the highest regard for him as a man and a teacher.' But that Sion Jenkins cheated in the first instance is an inescapable fact.

Much of the newspaper coverage at the time implied that a job-cheat like Sion Jenkins was capable of the worst of crimes. But cheating of that kind does not make a man a murderer. In considering Jenkins' guilt the business of his falsified qualifications has no place.

As to the other charges, Jenkins has admitted to hitting his wife in the early days of marriage. But there is no evidence that this was either frequent or alarmingly violent. And Lois was no meek and timid victim: she was then, as she has proved to be since, a woman of independent views and a strong will.

Much was also made of Jenkins caning and slapping his children but Lottie, when interviewed by the police, rejected this as she also rejected any suggestion that her father was violent towards her mother.

As for the suggestions of affairs with other women, even were these correct, they would not automatically make him into the *Sun's* sex-fiend. But it has to be added that no firm evidence of any philandering has emerged despite the most earnest attentions of the police and press.

So, what about his demeanour in the first hours after the discovery of the body? What was he doing sitting in the car when the ambulance men arrived? Why did he fail to offer first aid to the girl? How was it that he appeared so calm and collected when dealing with his daughters? Jenkins will say that when he found the body he was torn between consoling two hysterical children and seeing what could be done for Billie-Jo and making telephone calls. He had for the children's sake to remain calm. 'I had Billie-Jo dying on one side of the house. I had the children on the other, crying and screaming. I was running between them. You don't have any understanding of what it was actually like in that house when I returned', he said at his trial. And guilty or no, he was in shock. For less than a minute he had gone out to the car while waiting for the ambulance to park. Not really appropriate in the circumstances, one might say. Or, one might say, not rational but perfectly understandable for a man in shock.

Whilst the matter of timing does not prove conclusively Sion Jenkins' innocence, it does cast a huge shadow of doubt over the verdict. Go back to the trip in the car when Jenkins and Annie went to pick up Lottie from her clarinet lesson. When they left, Billie-Jo was painting the patio doors. They took Lottie's friend home to Elphinstone Road. The girl's mother had been waiting for her daughter, watching the clock. She was adamant that Jenkins arrived at her house at 3.15 pm.

Telephone records show that Jenkins made his first telephone call asking for an ambulance at 3.38 pm. In the 23 minute period between leaving Elphinstone Road at about 3.15 pm, he had driven home, a journey taking approximately four and a half minutes. Then after a brief stop in the house he had taken Annie and Lottie to Do It All. The journey there and back took an estimated quarter of an hour and they reached home shortly before 3.38 pm when Jenkins phoned for an ambulance.

If the two car journeys total nineteen and a half minutes, then they were in the house, after returning from Elphinstone Road, for only three and a half minutes. Could Sion Jenkins have murdered Billie-Jo in that short interval?

It was the blood which clinched the case at Jenkins' trial. There was so much blood all over the murder scene. It has been described as 'appallingly messy.' Remember the police surgeon? He said he had never seen anything so horrific. There was blood on the walls, on the dining-room floor, on the trellis and on the newly painted patio doors. Billie-Jo lay in a pool of blood. The tent peg beside her was covered with blood. So much blood. But why was Jenkins not obviously bloodstained? Had he in that brief period of time washed away all the signs of what he had done? Were there no visible splashes on his clothing, on his shirt, his pullover, his fleece, his trousers? Why were there only three blood stains on his right sleeve? He was right-handed and one might expect that that sleeve would have been heavily bloodied. And when they went on the trip to Do It All, did neither of the girls see any signs of blood on their father? Weren't his sleeves stained? Presumably as the murderer raised the tent peg over his head time after time to shatter Billie-Jo's skull some drops of blood would flick down onto his back. Did no blood from the weapon fall obliquely onto the back of Jenkins' fleece? What about Denise Franklin? Did she not see any obvious stains? Didn't the ambulance men note anything? Or the policemen? Would the murderer of Billie-Jo, who also might well have pieces of tissue, brain and bone on his clothing, not have been obvious to the people he came into contact with in the early stages of the investigation? This was a blood bath and the murderer was surely spattered, stained, saturated with his victim's blood.

Forensic examination found bloodstains only under the microscope. At appeal the defence introduced scientific evidence which showed that three drops of blood could be fragmented into 2000 droplets which could be exhaled strongly enough to reach Jenkins as he held Billie-Jo. Whilst the appeal judges acknowledged this evidence as 'relevant and credible' they still dismissed the appeal.

And then there are further doubts. Even if he had been bold enough when the girls were in the house with him or wild enough in the heat of the moment to commit such a murder, would not the girls, Annie and Lottie, have heard something?

On the day after the murder both children made video statements to the police. Annie said that when they left for Do It All she spoke to Billie-Jo. She also said that when she was cleaning out the utility room she had placed three tent pegs on top of the coal bunker at the side of the house. Did someone come in by the side gate after they had left for Do It All and pick up the tent peg? Lottie's statement strengthens the possibility of this: she said that the gate to the side passage of the house was closed when they left but open when they returned.

But the children's evidence was never presented in court. The police had spoken to the girls several times since their first statement and had told them that their father had murdered Billie-Jo and that he had lied about his professional qualifications. As a result, the defence decided not to call Annie and Lottie, fearing that their testimony had been contaminated.

Now to the weapon on the coal bunker. Why would Jenkins have gone to the coal bunker up the passage at the side of the house when there were other heavy implements nearer to hand? If it was a spur of the moment attack, would he not have taken up something close by? But an outsider, coming in by the side door would see the tent pegs there, ready.

And what about the journey to Do It All? Was it really an attempt to create an alibi? Surely Jenkins would have prolonged the journey even more had he wished to give the impression that an intruder had come into the house. This car trip, even if it was prolonged, lasted only fifteen minutes. Why did he not find some excuse to extend their absence from home even further? And the already open bottle of white spirit found in the house seems to be of minor importance. People do buy items they do not need, forgetting what lies in the remoter recesses of cupboards and drawers. And as for Jenkins forgetting his wallet, the prosecution cited this as proof that he had no intention of making any purchase at Do It All. But do we not all forget our wallets, our purses, sometimes?

And what about the prowler, the suspicious figure spotted by many witnesses in Lower Park Road that day? Was this the man that Margaret Barnett, who lived in Lower Park Road, told the police about? On the afternoon of the murder, at about 3.30, she heard a man cursing and making strange noises in the undergrowth on the other side of her garden fence. He eventually ran off. She reported this but was not called to give evidence.

Was this the local man renowned for threatening and violent behaviour, the man whose parents admitted to police that he was 'getting worse over the past year'? On the day of the murder he was seeking accommodation in Lower Park Road. The day before in Debenhams his odd behaviour had drawn staff's attention. Billie-Jo had been in Debenhams that day too. Had he seen her there? Had he followed the attractive 13 year old?

After the murder the man was traced. When police went to his flat they found that he had disposed of most of his clothing. His psychiatrist refused to allow police to question him. The man had been in a very disturbed state at the time of the murder and now could recall nothing of the events of that day.

But shortly after this the investigation turned away from prowlers. Now came the news that there were tiny spots of blood on Jenkins' clothing. And after that came the arrest, the trial ...

So who murdered Billie-Jo on the first spring-like day of 1997? Was it the man who now serves a life-sentence, who continues to protest his innocence, whose appeal to the European Court of Human Rights has been rejected as inadmissible and who now awaits the result of a review by the Criminal Cases Review Commission. Was it Sion Jenkins or some other? Is Sion Jenkins, whose daughters still write to him regularly, really one of the most brutal Sussex villains? Or does he not deserve that title?

Has the real murderer of Billie-Jo not yet been found?

RAZORS AND RACES

--------❁--------

If they had not been so comprehensively outwitted at Lewes on 18th June 1936, Jimmy Spinks and his Hoxton Mob might have taken over the racecourse protection racket in southern England. As it was, Darby Sabini from Clerkenwell's Little Italy wiped out the Hoxton boys without raising a finger. Only to be expected of course. 'Compared to Darby Sabini,' it has been said, 'all other British gang leaders have been merely messenger boys'. And it was on Lewes racecourse, that most modest of tracks – closed, alas, since 1964 – that the Hoxton Mob met its end and the power of all other racecourse gangs was weakened.

In *Lewes Remembers Racing and Race Days* the father of one contributor, then a child, spoke to Darby Sabini at the White Hart. The little man with the razor scarred face gave the child half a crown. How the small kindnesses of ruthless villains are so often fondly recalled.

Jimmy Spinks, Sabini's younger rival, a huge, powerful man, whose face, criss-crossed by razor scars, resembled 'a map of the London Underground', has been described by his great nephew, Lennie McClean, as a man who helped old ladies over roads and frequently slipped them a few quid. Truly soft hearted, we are invited to think. But there was another side to Jimmy Spinks's character. On one occasion, when asked to pay for his fish and two penn'orth, he is reputed to have thrown the shop cat in the frier.

This, then, is the class of men we are dealing with.

For years gangs had fought for the privilege of 'looking after' bookmakers at their trackside pitches. Sometimes mobs numbering up to sixty, armed with hatchets and bricks, knives and knuckledusters, battled on the courses. But by 1920, Darby

Sabini, under the cover of the so-called 'Bookmakers and Backers Racecourse Protection Society', controlled most of the southern tracks, his men guarding the bookmakers' stands, their hammers visible to any who might think of disputing their fiefdom.

The Jockey Club constantly complained that its gate-keepers were unable to keep out the gangs, fearing that if they tried to do so their faces would be sliced with razors or their collar bones smashed with hatchets. And the general public was outraged at the violent manner in which gangsters governed the tracks and gambling throughout the country. A Cardiff bookmaker was killed in his office and another from Sheffield was murdered in the street; in Tottenham Court Road there was another gang-related murder. There were fights on race-trains – a jockey was nearly thrown onto the Brighton line by a gang enraged at his winning a race – and in Brighton's streets men battled with razors, coshes, iron bars and bottles.

Matters had gone too far and eventually the Home Secretary, Sir William Joynson Hicks, determined to smash the power of the gangs. And when Jimmy Spinks and his boys turned up at Lewes races to take on their rivals, they were defeated, not by the weapons of the Italian Mob but by the waiting police. Only one Sabini ally, the bookie Alfie Solomon, a Jewish tearaway, was seen on the track that day and when he and his clerk were savagely assaulted, the police came out of hiding and arrested several of their attackers. The power of the Hoxton Mob was over. But how had it come about?

The immediate cause of the fight, it is said, was the 'chivving' (razor-slashing) of a Hoxton man by one of the Sabini gang at Liverpool Street station. A revenge attack was inevitable. Darby Sabini knew that Jimmy Spinks would not let the matter rest. It was when he heard on the grapevine that Spinks intended to come to Lewes races in force that Sabini put his plan into operation. An anonymous telephone call was sent to Chief Inspector 'Nutty' Sharpe, head of the Flying Squad. 'It's going to be off at Lewes on Monday,' Sharpe was told and he understood precisely what that cryptic statement meant. At the same time all of the Sabini bookies, with the exception of Solomon, were warned not to appear at the course on 8th June, the first day of the Lewes meeting.

Sharpe contacted the local police forces and from all over Sussex detectives and uniformed men in plain clothes waited on the course for the arrival of Spinks and his gang. At about 12.45 pm, an hour or so before the first race, a gang of 30 men emerged from the car park. For the next ten minutes as they sauntered round the three shilling ring, apparently looking for Sabini's men, they were shadowed by Inspector Stripp, Detective Sergeant Collyer and Detective Constable Janes, all from the Brighton police force. But where were the Sabinis? Some of the Hoxton men perhaps began to suspect a plot. One of them was heard to comment, 'It's no good here, boys. Too many top hats [plain clothes policemen].' But then a punter, Douglas Clayton of Beddingham, heard a shout: 'There they are. Let them have it, boys.'

They had spotted Alfie Solomon, carrying his equipment to his pitch. The gang surged towards him. Jimmy Spinks drew a hatchet from under his coat. Others brandished hammers, iron bars, sticks, truncheons, coshes, jemmies, billiard cues. One among them wielded what looked like part of a car axle. In seconds they surrounded Solomon, showering blows on his head. But the bookmaker was a brawler too, used to forays of this kind. He managed to wriggle through the mass and escape. His little clerk, Mark Frater, was less fortunate. Spinks's hatchet smashed through his bowler hat. 'Let him have it, boys,' he shouted.

One of the gang pinioned the clerk's arms and he was clubbed several times on the back of the head before falling to the ground, bleeding profusely. Then the fallen man was brutally kicked.

But by now, the police had come out of cover, blowing their whistles and joining the fray. 'Here they are, boys,' one of the gang called out. 'Blow.' Leaving Frater unconscious on the ground, the gang ran off in the direction of the car park, throwing away their weapons.

Although five of the gang, including Spinks, had been almost immediately apprehended, several had reached two cars and tried to drive away. One of the cars was quickly stopped and its occupants arrested. The second car, a Standard Sports, raced off down hill from the car park but was obliged to pull up to avoid a horse-box. Inspector Stripp then stood in front of the car calling out to the driver, 'You have just come from the car park.'

'We've only just got here and I took the wrong turning,' the driver answered. One of the five passengers added, 'Not us. We've only just come.'

But Stripp was not put off. 'You are members of that gang and I shall hold you here,' he said.

He was joined by Sergeant Collyer who stood on one running board while the Inspector took up his position on the other. The men were told to drive to the lock-up.

Some of the other men insisted that they had just arrived at the races. They had been in no trouble. Why were they being arrested? One, George Churchill who sold fruit at racetracks, said that no sooner had he arrived than he saw some people running towards him and, in trying to get out of the way, he had fallen into a ditch. The policeman who gave evidence said that when he found Churchill the man told him that he was only resting. 'Come and rest with me then,' the constable told him.

Another of the defendants told the policeman who had caught up with him, 'All right, all right. I haven't done anything.'

'What are you running away for then?' was the not unreasonable reply.

In the next half hour the police rounded up about twenty suspects. They were taken to the lock-up on the race hill and later to the police station. Frater, falling in and out of consciousness, was sent to Victoria Hospital in Lewes where his wounds were found to be less serious than had at first been feared. His bowler hat had saved him. Alfie Solomon had received only glancing blows and was treated as an outpatient.

At Sussex Assizes before Mr Justice Hilbery, sixteen men appeared, charged with the malicious wounding of Mark Frater with intent to do him grievous bodily harm and with riotously assembling together and assaulting Alfred Solomon and Frater. All pleaded not guilty. Their close friends had subscribed £1,000 towards their defence by first-class lawyers. Solomon, observing the underworld code, claimed to know nothing about what had happened and was not called to testify and Frater was too terrified to say much.

The key witness was, of course, Mark Frater, the 34 year old bookie's clerk. For two weeks after the fracas he had disappeared and he did not appear at the Magistrates Court. After being traced, however, he was called as a witness at the Assizes. He was willing to say no more than that he had been assaulted but he claimed not to recognise any of those in the dock. He denied knowing who had attacked him; said that he had no quarrel with anyone; swore that nobody had ever threatened him.

Frater recalled seeing some men approaching as he and Solomon reached the corner of the three-shilling ring. But shortly afterwards he was hit on the head and could remember nothing more. He had known Spinks, he said, for two or three years, meeting him at dog tracks, and had never had a quarrel with him.

For the prosecution, John Flowers told the jury, 'I submit to you that he was absolutely terrified of giving evidence of identification against any one of these men.'

Hadn't he been approached by Spinks before the Magistrates Court hearing, the bookies clerk was asked. Hadn't Spinks said to him, 'You don't recognise me, do you?' And as a result hadn't Frater disappeared shortly after?

'Not at all,' the poor man replied.

For the defence, Mr J.D. Cassels KC, asked Frater, 'Have you met Spinks since the hearing at the police court?'

'We had a drink together at Harringay and I asked Spinks if he was the man who was in trouble,' Frater answered. 'He said he was.'

'Did Spinks say that he did not know it was you who had been hit?'

'Yes.'

'Has any threat of any kind been made against you in connection with this case?'

'No.'

'Have you any fear of giving evidence today?'

'No, sir.'

So spoke a terrified man.

Asked about Albert Blitz, the 24 year old lorry driver and tic-tac man who had held him while Spinks and others had laid into him, Frater denied seeing him at Lewes.

For his part, Blitz said he did not know Frater, adding that in any case he was nowhere near where the assault took place. He had just left an eel stall when the police arrested him.

In cross-examination, Blitz said he did not know that in 1924 Solomon had been charged with the murder of a gangster-bookmaker called Barnet Blitz where the defence counsel had obtained a verdict of manslaughter. Albert claimed not even to have heard of his namesake nor of his knifing. Odd that this was not pursued further. Can there have been so many East End Blitzes involved in crime and bookmaking?

Jimmy Spinks, that ferocious man, admitted that he knew Frater well but denied taking part in the attack on him. Nor had he known that Frater had disappeared. The hatchet? No, he had never seen it before but in any case he would never dream of using such a weapon. He had never been to Lewes before and he was not a member of any race gang.

In the end, however, the jury believed the police evidence and found each of the sixteen prisoners guilty on both charges. All but three of the accused had previous serious convictions.

Pronouncing sentence, Mr Justice Hilbery commented, 'By the mercy of Providence, Frater was not killed ... I say by the mercy of Providence ... I perhaps ought to add also, through the alertness of the police and the prompt execution by the police of their duty. It certainly was not through any mercy that any one of you was disposed to show your victim.'

Criminals guilty of gang violence, using such 'villainous weapons', he continued, would be shown no mercy. He intended to hand down sentences that he hoped would demonstrate that crimes of violence did not pay.

Spinks, described by the judge as 'a desperate and dangerous man,' was given five years; Blitz four years and the others all received sentences ranging from three years to eighteen months.

It was a crushing blow to the racecourse gangs. Spinks's aim to run the racing underworld ended at Lewes. But even Darby Sabini, in destroying the opposition, served to weaken his own position too as Mr Justice Hilbery's sentences were an effective deterrent. He retained power in the East End for some years but eventually retired to Hove. He died in 1950, shattered by the death of his son, an RAF wartime pilot.

A question remains. There can be little doubt that it was Darby Sabini's tip-off to the police that led to the wholesale arrest of the

Hoxton Mob. But why did he fail to warn his old ally, Alfie Solomon, of what was about to occur? Why was Solomon the only man with Sabini links on the course that day? Was it that after long years supporting Jewish gangs and bookies Sabini had tired of them? Was Solomon, leader of the so-called Yiddisher Mob, no longer to be trusted? After all, when Alfie Solomon was charged with the death of Barnet Blitz in 1924 it was Sabini who had sought out and paid the master defence counsel, Sir Edward Marshall Hall, to defend him. And he did so successfully. But by 1936, it seems that Solomon was hung out to dry.

And when during his retirement years in Hove, Darby Sabini served his first prison sentence on a receiving charge, it is possible that he was framed by Alfie Solomon.

But that slight affray at Lewes was a mighty blow which did much to break up the racecourse gangs and to shatter their grip on the Sport of Kings. Though not entirely eradicated, violence at the racetracks of Britain was considerably reduced thereafter.

THE CHICKEN RUN

---❁---

The Camerons were worried. They had heard nothing from Elsie since she left the house the previous Friday. Quite unlike her to stay away for five days without notifying them. They knew that she had gone down to Crowborough to see Norman as she did most week-ends but they'd expected her back by now. She was a worry to them, Elsie with her 'nerves'. She couldn't even hold a job down. Hadn't worked for six months. She'd had a perfectly good post as a typist but after nine years they had got rid of her. Two or three other jobs followed but they hadn't kept her on. Elsie and her 'nerves'. At least she had a good hard-working fiancé. But where was she? And then there were the letters from Norman addressed to Elsie. They hadn't opened them but it was mysterious. Why was he writing to her? She was supposed to be down there in Sussex with him.

On 10th December Duncan Cameron sent a telegram to Norman. 'Elsie left Friday. Have heard no news. Has she arrived?' On the same day they received a reply: 'Not here. Open letters. Cannot understand.'

Alarmed, the Camerons read the first of the two letters, written on Sunday. 'My own darling Elsie … Well, where did you get to yesterday?' the writer asked. 'I went to Groombridge and you didn't turn up.' The second letter, written on the Monday, read, 'I was expecting a letter today, especially after not seeing you.'

Mr Cameron went at once to his local police station at Kensal Rise in North London. In consequence Norman Thorne received a visit from PC Beck of Crowborough. He was as mystified as the Camerons, Thorne told the policeman. He couldn't throw any light on the matter. But he'd do all he could to help, naturally, because she was his fiancée, had been for the past two years.

Thorne told Constable Beck that on the afternoon of Friday 5th December he had cycled to Tunbridge Wells and bought a pair of shoes and a chess set. From five o'clock until nearly ten o'clock he had been at the farm and then had gone to meet a local girl, Bessie Coldicott, and her mother, at Crowborough station and had escorted them home. He had come back to the farm at about 11.30 pm.

The next day, he said, he had gone to meet Elsie at Groombridge station but she had not turned up as arranged. He had written to her at her home and her parents were as surprised as he, especially as they said that Elsie had left for Crowborough on the Friday.

The day after speaking to PC Beck, Thorne went to the police station with a photograph of the missing 26 year old. From then on he was a constant worried visitor there, asking if there was any news. But there never was.

For the past two years Norman Thorne had been trying to build up the Wesley Poultry Farm at Blackness with £100 borrowed

Norman Thorne standing in the chicken run at Crowborough

from his father. He was a qualified electrical engineer but in the post-1918 slump he had lost his job in Kensal Rise. And here he was now struggling against the odds to make a go of things. But it was hard. Eggs and chicks weren't selling. At least his weren't. Perhaps it was because it was just that bit too remote from the centre of Crowborough. Maybe that was it. But it was dispiriting. After all his hard work. He'd built the pens and in the middle of them he'd even built the tiny, 7´ x 12´ hut he lived in. Scarcely room to swing a cat, just enough room for a trestle bed, a small table, a home-made bookshelf and a rickety chair.

At week-ends Elsie came down, often staying at the cottage of his neighbours. Both had been regular attenders at the Methodist chapel at Kensal Rise, both were members of the Band of Hope and he had been a Sunday School teacher there. And it was their intention to marry. They had been engaged for two years, since Christmas 1922. But Norman wanted things to be right financially. And at the moment they were not.

And to tell the truth, Elsie was rather a worry to him. It wasn't the fact that she was rather plain behind her wire-rimmed spectacles. It wasn't that she was really rather lack-lustre. It was the business of her 'nerves', the bouts of rage, the outbursts of tears, the hysterics. She had even suggested suicide.

There is always a dead period for newspapers, when there are no good stories. Editors cast around for something to excite the readers. And in early January 1925, the desperate editor of the *Daily News* sent one of his reporters down to Crowborough to see if there was anything in this business about a missing girl. Might be a decent story. Well, it was a good story, good enough to prompt other newspapers to send their reporters down to the chicken farm.

And Thorne's reactions did seem newsworthy. He did imply more than once that something unpleasant might have happened to her. 'Something dreadful must have happened, I feel sure of it,' he told reporters. 'Why should she commit suicide or run away when we were looking forward to a happy married life together?'

At the time the reporters thought his response different from usual. So many people whom they question in such circumstances are resentful, often aggressive. Not Norman Thorne. He was only too willing to talk. But there were times when he seemed unemotional, cold, unaffected really. It was odd, the sort of things he said. There was the occasion when he picked up an Indian club in his hut and said in jest – in jest? – 'Perhaps they think I killed her with this club and buried her there,' and he pointed at the chicken run nearest the gate. And there was another time when he suggested a particular spot in the same poultry run where they might photograph him – 'What about here?' he asked. 'Feeding the chickens?' In the light of what was to transpire it does seem ghoulish.

And then a couple of witnesses turned up, two nurserymen, who recalled seeing a girl near the farm gate going into the farm on the Friday afternoon. And there was a bus conductor who had his memory jogged and remembered a girl on the bus who seemed to answer the missing girl's description. And then in the first week of January, a month after Elsie's disappearance there was yet another witness, Mrs Annie Price, who remembered seeing a girl near the farm at the time in question.

It was at this point, on 11th January, that the Chief Constable of East Sussex called in Scotland Yard. Chief Inspector John Gillan, who enjoyed an enormously high reputation, arrived in Crowborough. He was assisted in this investigation by Superintendent Isaac Budgen of Uckfield and Inspector George Edwards of Crowborough. Gillan made no attempt to see Thorne until 14th January. Then he visited the shed, Norman Thorne's cramped squalid world with its delapidated furniture, its home-made radio, its rusty fire grate, its book-case holding, unsurprisingly, engineering books and, surprisingly, pathology books. And in the corner an Indian club.

In the course of the day the shed was searched. There was a bundle of letters which Gillan was satisfied indicated motive for what might have happened to Elsie. Those written at the end of November 1924 were enough to convince Gillan that Norman Thorne could provide the answer to the mystery.

The police found a letter written to Elsie by Thorne himself which is interesting. On 25th November he says to her: 'There are one or two things I haven't told you … It concerns someone else … I am afraid I am between two fires.' He asks her to send this letter back to him and says she should keep quiet about it.

On 26th November Elsie replied to his letter which presumably enclosed as he had requested. She said that she expected him to arrange their marriage as soon as possible. 'This worry is very bad for the baby ... I feel sick every day and things will soon be noticeable to everybody, and I want to be married before Christmas ... I really think an explanation is due to me over all this.'

So, she was pregnant.

The next day Thorne answered: 'What I haven't told you is that on certain occasions a girl has been here late at night ... When you gave in to your nerves again and refused to take interest in life I gave up hope in you and let myself go ... She thinks I am going to marry her, of course, and I have a strong feeling for her or I shouldn't have done what I have.'

Now he is telling Elsie that her rival is pregnant. Her rival who lives in Crowborough is Bessie Coldicott.

Elsie fires off the next letter on 28th November. 'You have absolutely broken my heart. I never thought you were capable of such deception,' she says. 'You are engaged to me and I have first claim on you ... Oh Norman, I wouldn't have believed it of you. It's a poor thing for a man to let himself go because his girl has her nerves bad ... Well, Norman, I expect you to marry me and finish with the other girl, and as soon as possible. My baby must have a name.'

The search of the farm went on. In the toolshed police found some cheap jewellery, a bracelet and a broken wrist-watch. And digging in the potato patch the police unearthed an attache case containing a pair of shattered spectacles and a baby's frock.

Thorne was now charged with murder. The remains of Elsie Cameron were somewhere on the farm, the police were certain. On 15th January, digging by oil lamp in the chicken run nearest the gate, the mud oozing over their boots, they unearthed a biscuit box. Its contents were wrapped in sacking and they were so tightly packed that they had to be forced out of the box. When it was opened they found the head of Elsie Cameron.

Lower down they found three more parcels in sacking – the torso with the upper limbs attached and the legs in separate bundles. Rings and a birthmark helped to confirm the body as that of Elsie Cameron.

As there was no transport available at such an early hour, the body was conveyed in Thorne's wheelbarrow by two policemen and two local men to the undertaker's mortuary. Story-hungry journalists from the national dailies turned up just in time to photograph the unseemly cortege.

In his statement Thorne admitted dismembering the body but he insisted that he had not killed her.

Elsie, he said, came down to Crowborough without any warning on the Friday. She had arrived in the late afternoon and had spent hours in the shed arguing about his unfaithfulness and about Bessie Coldicott. She insisted on staying the night. Finally, at about 9.30 pm Thorne had left her in the shed because he had arranged to pick up Bessie and her mother who had been to Brighton and to walk home with them. And that is what he had done.

The statement continues: 'She remained in the hut with the dog … When I returned about half past eleven, the dog came down to meet me. When I opened the hut door I saw Miss Cameron hanging from a beam by a piece of cord as used for the washing line. I cut the cord and laid her on the bed. She was dead. I then put out the lights. She had her frock off and her hair was down … I was about to go to Dr Turle and knock up someone to go for the police and I realised the position I was in.'

Thorne had then stripped her completely and burned her clothes in the fire.

Then he had laid sacks on the floor. 'I got my hacksaw … I sawed off her legs, and the head, by the glow of the fire.'

In the early hours he had buried the parts.

She had kept telling him she was pregnant, his statement goes on, and he did not believe her. In June 1923, he says, 'we became on intimate terms, that is feeling one another's person and from that it went that I put my person against hers, but in my opinion I did not put it into her. This practice continued on almost all the occasions when Miss Cameron came to the hut. We had previously made up our minds that she should not become pregnant.'

Thorne stuck to this account throughout. He had not killed her. He had disposed of the body simply in panic.

At the five-day trial held at Lewes and beginning on 11th March 1925 before Mr Justice Finlay the medical evidence hinged on one question – did Elsie Cameron die by hanging? In other words, did she commit suicide? Thorne claimed that he saw distinct rope marks on her throat.

Both prosecution and defence agreed she died at the farm; both agreed that Thorne had lied to cover up her death and both agreed that he had dismembered her. Both teams were of the opinion that the cause of death was not hanging. But the Crown team, led by Sir Henry Curtis-Bennett KC, maintained that she had been beaten and had as a result died of shock while the defence, led by Mr J.D. Cassels KC, stuck out for suicide by partial hanging and ensuing shock.

Sir Bernard Spilsbury, the Home Office pathologist, who first saw the body on 17th January, two days after it was exhumed, said that there was bruising to the face, head and legs. The two last blows had left massive damage to the forehead, reducing the tissues to pulp. Spilsbury said that there was nothing to suggest that she had hanged herself. There was no rope burn or bruise on her neck. This was supported by Gillan who said that the beam bore no rope marks and that it was covered with undisturbed dust. He had experimented with a rope and an attached weight. When the weight dropped it left a groove in the wood.

For the defence Dr Robert Bronte seriously challenged Spilsbury. He had seen Elsie Cameron's body in a state of advanced decomposition, much changed by water, in February after it was again exhumed, this time at Willesden cemetery. He stated he saw creases on the neck which he said were from strangulation. Spilsbury countered this, saying that such creases were found naturally on women's necks.

In his summing up Mr Justice Finlay was to defer to Spilsbury's opinion, 'undoubtedly the very best that can be obtained.'

Thorne himself made a poor impression on the jury. His matter-of-fact description of the dismemberment appalled them. His failure to offer a convincing reply to an apparently innocuous question from Curtis-Bennett told heavily against him. 'If your story is correct, when you went out at half past nine,' the prosecutor asked, 'did she still believe that you were going to marry her if she was pregnant?'

'Yes.'

'Then why should she commit suicide?'

In the dock Norman Thorne had no answer. Nor could he explain how her watch and spectacles were damaged or why he burnt her dress and jumper. Why, if he was innocent, had he lied so?

He was just trying to help himself, he said, 'trying to build up evidence that I knew nothing about Miss Cameron's death ... I had gone so far and I could not stop ... One lie led to another'.

And in fact they led to the gallows.

So let's just consider one or two other factors. Take the dismemberment first. Some say that Thorne was planning his defence from the time he started cutting up the body. You see, he did not cut across the throat. He took off the head as close to the shoulders as possible. Why? Presumably to keep the neck intact because he believed it would show the marks of hanging. But what if she did not hang? After death did he place a rope round her neck just to create marks? If so, he was sadly mistaken. Had he read those pathology books on his shelves rather more closely he might have learnt that such marks, imposed after death, fade completely.

And consider his behaviour after 5th December. The next day it was a trip to the cinema with Bessie who incidentally, and despite what he had hinted at in his letter to Elsie, was not pregnant. But then, come to think of it, neither was Elsie, according to Spilsbury. And what about the jokes with the photographers? What about his choosing to have his photograph taken exactly where he had dug his fiancée into the ground?

And what about the newspaper cuttings found in the shed? These referred to Patrick Mahon who less than a year earlier had stood in the same dock at Lewes on a charge of murdering and dismembering his girl-friend at the Crumbles at Eastbourne. Had he read these in order to learn from Mahon's errors? Certainly he did not go to the dreadful extremes employed by Mahon to get rid of the body.

And wonder about this. For how long, do you think, had Norman Thorne been planning to do away with his tiresome, endlessly nagging fiancée? Weeks? Months?

Yet, all in all, he was not basically a wicked man. But faced with one problem, how to escape the constant nuisance to him that Elsie had become, he followed a wicked path. If only he had never met her, if only he had met Bessie earlier, if only ...

BUYING A POLICEMAN

—————— ❀ ——————

Alan Bennett had had enough. They kept coming back for more cash. He wouldn't put up with it any longer. He went to Scotland Yard. And perhaps no one there was very surprised. There had been odd rumours for years about bribery and corruption in the Brighton police force. Time to investigate.

There were all sorts of people who could help. There was Sammy Bellson, for example, club owner and bookmaker, not overly trustworthy, but a man with something to say. He met two of the investigating officers out of town, out near the racecourse, away from the smoky clubs with their dodgy deals, their raucous clamour, away from the town's violent, dangerous edge.

'One of the worst cases I know about', Bellson said, 'is a woman doing 15 months for abortion. Her name is Brabiner. The one who can tell you all about it is Betty Lawrence. There's someone else you ought to see – that's old Harry Leach who lives in Stanford Avenue. They did his son over some jewellery. Ridge sent me along to do some business with him. I went but Leach would not pay enough and later Ridge himself went. You see him and his son. They can help you.'

Ridge sent Bellson to do some business? Ridge, Brighton's Chief Constable, sent this dubious bookie on police business? What was this?

Within days the first arrest was made. On 18th October 39 year old Detective Sergeant Trevor Heath, a CID man for ten years, was taken into custody for trying to extort £50 from Alan Bennett whose complaint had led to the investigation; on 25th October came the arrests of Detective Inspector John Hammersley, second in charge of CID, along with Anthony James Lyons, manager of Sherry's Bar and, of all people, the Chief Constable himself,

Alan Bennett

Charles Ridge. Some weeks later, Sammy Bellson, who had offered such helpful information, was also arrested. All five were charged with conspiring together between 1st January 1949 and 18th October 1957, 'to obstruct the course of public justice in that Heath, Hammersley and Ridge acted contrary to their public duty as police officers in relation to the administration of the law'.

The case against these five men, revealed at the Magistrates Court at the end of 1957, and then in the Central Criminal Court in February 1958, was complex. How could it be otherwise with the guardians of the law in the dock and ranged against them several undoubted criminals? Had these policemen really made regular dishonest requests for cash, for 'fivers' and 'tenners', 'scores', 'ponies' (£25), 'halves' (£50) and 'tons' (£100)? Multiply those figures every time by 15 to get some idea of the value of the sums today.

James Swaby, 31, housebreaker and pimp, had been convicted 13 times. His wife, Sheila, had 50 convictions for soliciting. Another witness, Alice Brabiner, had just been released from her 15 month sentence. And other bit-part players, other petty criminals, were also to take the stand. The fruiterer and grocer, Ernest Waite, denounced in court as 'a scoundrel', was a receiver of stolen goods on a very large scale. The one-time chef and club owner Alan Bennett, also known as Brown, Woods or Ferguson, now a metal dealer with a home in Mayfair, wore Savile Row suits and drove a Rolls Royce. But he had convictions for receiving, burglary, theft and fraud, although he had not been in prison since 1949. He admitted in court to not having submitted Income Tax returns for some years. He took £40 a week from the takings for himself and, so he said, another £20 for the Chief Constable.

This cannot have seemed a very convincing prosecution witness line-up. Admittedly, Bellson had a prison record but the others had what appeared to be impeccable backgrounds. All three policemen had been in the Brighton force since before the war. After the navy, Heath returned to police duties and in 1955 made more arrests than any other detective constable in the force. Hammersley had been a major in the Military Police and had been mentioned in dispatches. Like Heath, he had 11 commendations. He had been promoted to Inspector in 1956. Charles Ridge had joined the Brighton Police in 1924. He had risen through the ranks to become Superintendent, then Deputy Chief Constable and finally in July 1956, Chief Constable. Tony Lyons, licensee and manager of Sherry's Bar since 1950, was a well-known Brighton figure with no criminal record.

Bellson had mentioned to the Scotland Yard men that the Leaches might be worth speaking to. John Leach who ran the Burlesque Club, a drinking club in West Street, had bought some rings, watches and gold coins from a customer, Michael Roberts. But they had been stolen from a jewellery shop in the town. Roberts was arrested and then Leach, protesting his innocence, had been drawn into the enquiries. In December 1954 Hammersley and Heath interviewed him in the presence of his father, Harry, a comfortably-off wholesale fish merchant. According to the detectives, Harry Leach had said to them, 'Now we are men of the world. Can't we settle this now?' He had put his hand in his pocket and there was a rustle of paper. Hammersley claimed to have said, 'Harry, you had better put that away before you make a bloody fool of yourself.'

The following day Ridge, at that time a Superintendent, had visited Harry Leach. His version was that he had gone there to give him good advice, to warn him to stay within the law.

Bellson's version was markedly different. He said that, at the urging of Ridge, he had called on the Leaches, telling them that the matter could be straightened out. Harry Leach had given him £100 but later Bellson had returned, saying, 'It's not enough. They only laughed at me.' The old man had then picked up the money saying, 'If that's no good, they can do their worst.' The officers were apparently asking for £250 'to throw the evidence in the sea.' John Leach was subsequently tried and found guilty but later released on appeal.

James Swaby, a man with a long criminal record, told the court that he had been in custody, facing charges of housebreaking, when Trevor Heath came to see him in the cells. Swaby said he was concerned that if the court knew that his last conviction was for living on his wife's immoral earnings his sentence would be severe. It was all up to him, Heath had told him. 'Come on, lad,' the detective had said, 'don't let's beat about the bush. You have been around.' Swaby had given the detective £10 but this was insufficient. When Sheila Swaby asked Heath later what her husband's chances were, he said he was willing to leave out all mention of 'living on immoral earnings' for a 'consideration'. He asked her how she was fixed for £50. But she was unable to come up with the cash.

Swaby was sentenced to five years. Heath had included the immoral earnings charge on Swaby's sheet, read out in court. Later, when Sheila Swaby met Heath, he said to her, 'You see what has happened? You didn't look after me so I didn't look after your husband.'

From prison Swaby wrote to Ridge, then Chief Constable, accusing Heath of conspiracy but there was no response.

One constable was to swear that he heard Heath suggest a sum of money to Swaby – a 'pony', he thought – though he did not, out of loyalty to his sergeant, report this. The constable also knew of the Chief Constable's high regard for Heath, one of his most successful detectives, and feared that in some way his own career might be jeopardised if he reported the matter.

During Swaby's trial, the constable said Heath had told him to go outside and ask Mrs Swaby if she had brought anything for him. When he returned and told Heath she had nothing, he was told to 'go outside with her again and tell her it is no good backing a horse after the off'.

Mrs Alice Brabiner was a back-street abortionist in the days when in Britain abortion was against the law. In November 1956 she performed an illegal operation on a girl in a flat belonging to a Mrs Betty Lawrence who also provided the syringe for the operation. This matter came to the attention of the police.

Heath called upon Mrs Brabiner, warning her that she faced 14 years in prison. The terrified woman offered him a few pounds to forget the matter. It was refused but then Heath came back to see her again. If she paid him, he told her, it would help her case. He could speak up for her in court, he said, but a few pounds were not enough. Later, Mrs Brabiner said, Lyons, the manager at Sherry's, came to see her and told her that it would cost her 'a ton'. Finally, Heath agreed that she could pay in instalments but when she asked if he would wait for some of her money until after the trial, Heath answered, 'You don't back a horse after the race.' By the time she came to trial at Lewes in April 1957, she had paid out £68, a huge sum by her standards.

Meanwhile Betty Lawrence who had supplied the syringe and in whose flat the operation had been carried out spoke to Heath. Would her name be in the papers, she asked. She was worried about what her husband would say. More worrying, however, was the prospect of being charged as party to the illegal operation. Well, Heath told her, he might be able to prevent her being prosecuted. He told her to see Lyons who allegedly said it would cost 'a ton'. That was too much, Mrs Lawrence said, but she could raise £25. There was further negotiation with Heath. 'The guv'nor is getting annoyed,' he told her. 'The guv'nor will want more than that.' Eventually they settled on £50.

After Mrs Brabiner's trial at which she was sentenced to 15 months' imprisonment, Heath met Mrs Lawrence in a public house where she handed over her last instalment of £10.

Before Ridge and the others appeared at the Magistrates Court hearing, it was revealed that Mrs Lawrence had received a threatening phone call, warning her that if she testified she 'would be cut up by Billy Howard's boys.' Who made the call was never discovered. Nevertheless, she did appear in the witness box.

But the fruiterer and grocer Ernest Waite had more astonishing tales to tell. He was a receiver of stolen goods in large quantities and his relationship with Hammersley and Heath and according to him, with Ridge, was close and deeply corrupt. In court, assured that he would not be prosecuted for his revelations, he admitted that between 1949 and September 1957 he dealt in stolen goods and that he, Hammersley and Heath had a 'gentleman's agreement'. Waite was told not to receive anything stolen in Brighton but he was given freedom of the town with regard to things outside Brighton. He was also warned by the detectives whenever any out-of-town property was 'iffy'. Hammersley and Heath also had contacts through whom Waite could move on some of his stolen goods. 'I was more or less made an agent,' Waite told the court. On one occasion Hammersley arranged for the disposal of a lorryload of bacon and butter for which he received £50. And there were other stories of huge hauls of tinned goods – tomatoes, corned beef, peaches, coffee. In effect Waite was being encouraged by policemen to act as a receiver of stolen goods.

Waite said that Hammersley used to call at his shop in New England Road every Saturday morning. He would help himself to two or three pounds of pears, grapes, bananas, tinned fruit, tins of cream, pineapples and maybe some bacon and chicken. Hammersley would hand over £1 or 10 shillings and then would wait for change. At Christmas time Waite usually gave Hammersley £10 and a turkey. In all, over the years, Waite said, he must have paid the detective over £200. As for Heath, in addition to goods, he had received about £50. Not that either detective ever asked for money. Rather, they dropped hints. On one occasion, when Heath talked about buying a new suit, Waite gave him £5. Waite said that he regarded it as a form of blackmail but considering the kind of service he was receiving from the policemen that seems a touch ungrateful.

Waite told the court about a butcher named Matheson who sold cat and dog meat in his shop which was a cover for black market meat. According to Waite, Ridge went there on Friday evenings for meat for which he did not pay. In return Matheson was always warned of the arrival of Ministry of Food inspectors.

In August 1957 one of the largest individual thefts on railway property took place at Bishopsgate railway goods yard. A consignment of one and a half million cigarettes went missing. Within two days they were offered to Waite who had been contacted by the thieves. When Waite told Hammersley about the cigarettes, the detective saw the potential. 'I think we will be on a good thing if we can get the cigarettes,' he said. 'We should get about £1,500 from the insurance company.'

It became known to the British Transport Police that the stolen cigarettes were being offloaded in Brighton but when Superintendent Moody of the BTP tried to make headway in the investigation he found Hammersley particularly unhelpful. Moody, a detective for 35 years, was to say that he had never encountered a case where progress was so slow. Eventually, without notifying the Brighton force, he sent his own men into town to make enquiries.

In court, Moody agreed with the Solicitor General that it was unusual to take such action. Indeed, he volunteered the description 'most discourteous'. So why then, he was asked, had he taken such a step.

'I no longer trusted the Brighton CID,' was the Superintendent's reply. Within days, he had searched Waite's house and the shop in New England Road and found tobacco and cigarettes. In Brighton police station Waite made a statement. Cracks in the wall were appearing.

And Alan Bennett had gone to Scotland Yard two months earlier with his story. The cosy corruption which had gone on for years was now about to crumble.

Bennett, a chef by training, a housebreaker by inclination, had since his release from prison in 1949 completely changed his fortunes. He and his wife had worked hard and from their now considerable bank balance bought the Astor Hotel. At Easter 1955 he opened the Astor Club in the converted basement. But business was slow: it was the licensing laws at fault. He had to shut at 10.30 pm when the night was just starting for real drinkers. Tony Lyons, an old acquaintance, called on Bennett, telling him that if he was not greedy, he would be able to stay open beyond normal closing time and not be bothered by the police. Later Lyons brought Ridge, then a Superintendent, to the club and there was a conversation about how much Bennett would have to pay. Lyons said that 'a score a week' would be all right. In court it was denied that 'the guv'nor' heard or took part in this conversation. Bennett spoke of payments made to Ridge for the next six or seven weeks. One witness stated that he saw Bennett in Sherry's giving a rolled-up newspaper containing £5 notes to a man resembling Ridge. Later Heath took over, calling for the weekly 'present from the club'.

The Astor Club now stayed open until three and four in the morning. Not that it was at all sedate. There was general rowdiness, fighting, drunkenness. Locally it was known as 'the Bucket of Blood'. Yet it was never successfully raided. Twice in 1955 Heath telephoned Mrs Bennett, warning her not to open the club on particular nights.

Mrs Blanche Cherryman, however, a resident at the Astor and occasional receptionist, was concerned at the way the club was being run. She went to see Ridge, telling him that she had taken an anonymous telephone message to close the club that night. 'Say it was Charlie,' the caller had said. Charles Ridge apparently made no comment when he was informed of this.

After only a few months at the Astor, Bennett tired of the pressures which Hammersley and Heath were putting on him. There was the business with Walker who came to stay at the Astor in July 1955. Walker was a thief on the run who had brought with him the takings of a very successful outing to East Anglia. But the law caught up with him and he was arrested dining in a restaurant with Bennett's wife. Bennett was anxious that his wife's name should not appear in the newspapers. Heath who called on him was more anxious to be given his 'whack of the grand' which Walker claimed had been stolen from his room. Bennett vehemently denied all responsibility for this but he gave Heath £30 to take care of the newspapers.

Whether Bennett's criminal career was totally over seems uncertain. A stolen cheque uttered by 'Austen Ferguson' – a name used by Bennett in the past – had turned up in Leeds. Bennett would have to go there, Heath told him. But after £15 exchanged hands, Leeds was never mentioned again.

In June 1956, after Bennett had sold the Ascot, he met Heath in Brighton. Bournemouth CID had been asking about him, Bennett was told. A jeweller's shop had been broken into and items valued at £6,000 had been stolen. Bennett was aggrieved. He had not been on any jobs, he told the detective. Nevertheless, he gave Heath £10 and agreed to go that evening to Brighton CID office where he was introduced to Hammersley. The Inspector told Heath to telephone Bournemouth. Heath left the office. 'Everything is all right,' he announced when he came back. He turned to Bennett. 'Don't forget John,' he said. Bennett, still claiming his innocence, was disgusted. He threw two screwed up £5 notes on the floor by Hammersley's chair and left. In fact, Heath had told Bournemouth police that he had interrogated Bennett to no avail and had said that he was now out of the country.

Perhaps the most bizarre moment in the relationship between the two men was when Heath suggested that Bennett break into Woolworth's. The detective said that he knew one of the managers who could furnish the keys. All Bennett had to do was open the safe and Heath would take a share of the proceeds. Outraged, Bennett said he had enough money of his own nowadays and did not need to go burgling.

The relationship between Heath and Bennett blew hot and cold. Bennett admitted to buying him some ties. On another occasion when Heath wanted money for a deposit on a car, Bennett paid £70 for a diamond ring which apparently belonged to Heath's wife. But why sell a ring to a man who was not a jeweller, he was asked in court, to a man who had a criminal record. Heath accepted that it was 'a little indiscreet'. Perhaps the truth was that he would get a more generous offer from a man over whom he had some measure of control.

Then Bennett learnt that there was a warrant out for him for 'a screwing job' in Folkestone. According to Heath, 'a half' would take care of it. And now Bennett realised that there was to be no end to the business. Heath and Hammersley and people like them would always be there. In July 1957 he went to Scotland Yard.

All sorts of other bits and pieces came out at the trial, all sorts of other questions. Why, for instance, had Hammersley and his wife gone on holiday to Paris with a convicted criminal? Even if Hammersley, Heath and Bellson were guilty, was Ridge simply being set up by a group of ruthless criminals? Was Lyons, like Bellson, a go-between or was he misunderstood? Could it be true that Ridge had no idea that the Astor Club had such a bad reputation, that it was open till the early hours? Did Mrs Cherryman, the receptionist, lie when she said that she had seen Ridge there late on several occasions? Was there not something odd in the fact that when Mrs Mason took over the Ascot and refused to make payments her club was raided and closed down? Why did Ridge not take up Mrs Cherryman's accusations that CID officers were not only taking money but also warning the Bennetts about planned raids?

And so on ... until 30th February 1958, when Hammersley and Heath were found guilty of conspiracy and were each sentenced to five years' imprisonment by Mr Justice Donovan. Sammy Bellson received three years.

Both Ridge and Lyons were acquitted.

Addressing the two policemen, the judge observed '... neither of you had that professional and moral leadership which both of you should have had and were entitled to expect from the Chief Constable of Brighton, now acquitted.'

Back in Brighton, Charles Ridge, within a year or two of retirement after a not totally undistinguished career, was dismissed by the Watch Committee which stated that he had been negligent in the discharge of his duty and was 'unfit for the same'.

There must be temptations sometimes in the work that such men do. They mix with criminals out of necessity. How else do they learn what is occurring in the criminal world? They need informants and sometimes out of gratitude or out of necessity, they shield them from criminal prosecution. Are they then colluding in crime when they do this? Are they then engaged in semi-criminal activities themselves? In which world do they belong, they must sometimes ask themselves. For some policemen in this situation, there is an inexorable slide into active criminality. This, it seems, explains in part what happened in Brighton.

FIELD AND GRAY

———— ❁ ————

They hadn't been open long when 'the boys', as the barmaid Dorothy Ducker called them, came in. Just after twelve on the Thursday when they turned up. Becoming quite regulars now at the Albemarle. Public bar, of course. They'd been coming in for the last few weeks, Jack and Billy, lunchtimes, afternoons, evenings. Not that they had all that much to spend. Cheapest beer, tuppence-halfpenny a pint or a threepenny-halfpenny bitter, sometimes. And for smokes, Woodbines, Gold Flake, nothing too expensive. But they are cheerful enough chaps. Jack, the young florid-faced one, doesn't say so much but he's really sharper than Billy who's always pulling Dorothy's leg. At one o'clock they're off to lunch and then, just before 2.30 pm closing time, they're back, just for 'a quick drink'.

'What about a buckshee one on the house?' Billy asks her, his South African vowels clipped.

They don't give drinks on tick, he's told. He should know that.

'Well,' he says, 'what about a biscuit for the dog?'

Over the top of the counter she sees the walking stick with the bulldog's head. Another of his jokes.

'You wait till this evening,' Billy tells her. 'We shall have some money by then.' And off they go.

On Monday 16th August 1920, Irene Munro, a London typist, came down to Eastbourne for a holiday. It was a nice place, select, safe for a young girl on her own, so her mother said. She found lodgings at 393 Seaside Road, almost at the beginning of that desolate two-mile stretch of beach called the Crumbles.

But perhaps the 17 year old was very lonely in this strange place. Perhaps for that reason Irene was glad of any company that turned up, glad to talk to a couple of men she wouldn't have bothered with in London.

Both men were unemployed. One of them, 19 year old Jack Field, had been dishonourably discharged from the navy the previous February. He had been in trouble with the police, had even served a jail sentence. Now he lived with his mother. The second man, the 28 year old South African, Billy Gray, a married man, had a war disability pension, and now walked with a limp.

Irene met the two men on the Tuesday when she walked with them to Beachy Head. On the following day they went to

The young Irene Munro

Pevensey Castle. And there she was on the Thursday afternoon, crossing the road from her lodgings to the Archery bus-stop to meet Jack and Billy. Not difficult to say why the men were attracted to the tall, good-looking girl with the dark brown hair and brown eyes.

Off they went towards Pevensey, all laughs and jokes, linking arms and in high old spirits, Irene in her black straw hat and her vivid green coat trimmed with imitation fur which she was wearing because it was so cold that August afternoon. They climbed the fence across to the cinder path and onto the long, bleak stretch of windswept shingle, walking along the railway track as far as the stationary railway carriage that the ballast workers used for a shelter. The girl smiled at the workmen sitting there. One of her companions looked in and made a cheery comment. They had picked up a cat along the way. They handed it to the workmen.

On they went, the three of them. But then, in the next quarter hour or so, the laughing stopped, the jokes and the chatting came to an end.

And something terrible happened.

It was early evening when 'the boys' came in to the Albemarle. They were in high spirits, excited, noisy. They ordered bottled beer and were smoking expensive Turkish cigarettes.

But Billy looked scruffy and Dorothy mentioned it to him. She'd never before seen him in anything other than his grey suit and here he was in this dark blue suit and dirty boots. Got his grey suit wet, he says. Jack had pushed him in the sea this afternoon. He'd been soaked and his grey suit wasn't dry yet.

Then off they went to the Hippodrome, to catch the first house starting at seven o'clock. And in the Hippodrome bar, during the interval, Billy repaid debts adding up to nine shillings to two of his pals. 'Have you been setting about somebody?' one of them asked in jest.

Back at 393 Seaside Road, Mrs Wynniatt was worried. She hadn't seen her lodger since early afternoon when she had popped in for her coat. It was past midnight when she gave up waiting for the girl and went to bed.

Willie Weller and his mother, on holiday from Lewisham, decided on the Friday to have a picnic on the Crumbles. And while Mrs Weller sat out of the wind, 13 year old Willie explored the beach until he tripped over a black-stockinged foot sticking out of the shingle. Alarmed, back to their digs went the Wellers, persuading their reluctant landlord, Clement Lamb, to return to the beach with them.

The spot where the boy had tripped was in a dip about 25 yards from the railway track. As soon as he reached the site, Mr Lamb saw the foot. He cleared away some of the shingle, revealed a battered face and horrified, covered it up again. He sent for the police who in turn sent for a doctor from nearby Westham.

Dr Cadman examined the girl's body where it lay under a thin shroud of shingle. There was a mask of blood over the hideously mutilated face. Both lower and upper jaws were fractured and several teeth were broken away. The left temple was bruised. Under the chin a triangular wound appeared to have been made with an instrument which had penetrated the roof of the mouth. The left eye was severely damaged and along the right ear was a long, incised wound. There were no signs of rape or attempted rape.

Dr Cadman calculated the probable time of death as not earlier than eleven o'clock on the Thursday night. It was a judgment which would be disputed in court in the succeeding months. He believed that the girl had been sitting down when she received the first head wounds from a fist. Then a stone had been picked up and thrown onto her head. He thought that the ferrule of a stick could have caused some of the lacerations.

On the Saturday morning, the local newspaper blazoned the story about an unknown girl found murdered on the Crumbles. But when Mrs Wynniatt opened her *Eastbourne Herald*, she knew who it was. Her lodger had now been missing for a second night. At once she and her husband went to the police station and were taken to the mortuary. The Wynniatts could not recognise the girl's massively damaged face. But they identified the clothing as Irene Monro's.

In the course of the day, Chief Inspector Mercer arrived from Scotland Yard to take over the investigation. He contacted the ballast workers who had been on the Crumbles on Thursday afternoon. They spoke of two men and a girl coming along the

track. The men had both worn grey suits, according to one
witness; another had an idea that one of them wore a blue suit.
The witnesses did agree, however, that one carried a walking stick
and the other had his arm round the girl's waist. And the girl in
the mortuary, that was the girl they had seen.

The Eastbourne police surgeon, James Adams, conducted the post-
mortem on the Saturday afternoon. Adams thought that a large,
bloodstained stone found near the body was the principal weapon.
He thought that some of the injuries had been caused by 'a broad
stick'. In contrast to the opinion of Dr Cadman, Adams' view was
that death occurred as early as Thursday afternoon. He was sure
that Irene could not have been alive as late as Thursday night.

Now that Irene had been identified as a lodger at 393 Seaside
Road, other witnesses came forward. A house painter had seen
her walking towards the Crumbles with two men. A plasterer
working on houses nearby saw the trio and recognised Gray
although he did not recognise either the other man or the girl.

One significant witness was Frederick Wells, an unemployed 26
year old, who went to the police station with his story on the
Monday. On the previous Thursday afternoon, he and his friend,
William Putland, on leave from the navy, saw two men and a girl
walking together towards the Crumbles and just because they had
nothing else to do, Wells and Putland decided to follow them.

Wells told the police that he and Putland had followed the three
nearly as far as the railway carriage. One of the men, Wells noted,
was carrying a stick with a carved head, a bulldog's head. And
then, they had decided to give up their pursuit and had turned
back to town.

Wells and Putland heard the news of the murder on the Crumbles
on the Sunday afternoon but failed to put two and two together.
Not until the Monday afternoon, after Putland had returned to his
ship, did Wells eventually turn up at the police station. He was
taken to the mortuary where he identified Irene by her hair.

On Tuesday 24th August, Wells accompanied Inspector Mercer
to the seafront. And there they were, Field and Gray, talking to
three girls. Wells was able to identify Field, the shorter of the two

Police pictures of Gray and Field

men, but was unsure about his companion. Nevertheless, both men were arrested and taken to the police station where a Detective Inspector greeted them with the words, 'I expect you wonder why you have been brought here.' Field replied, 'We have been expecting this as we both have been wearing grey suits.'

Field and Gray were in custody for two days during which time both made statements denying any responsibility for the Crumbles murder.

Jack Field said that on the Thursday afternoon he and Gray walked to Pevensey, passing the Crumbles on the way. They went into the castle grounds where they met a servant girl from Eastbourne called Maud Baxter. They left Pevensey at about four o'clock and walked back to town where they had an ice cream. They went to Gray's house and played cards and in the evening they went to the Hippodrome.

The next day, after a morning on the seafront, they went to the Tivoli cinema in the afternoon and in the evening to the Central cinema. After this they had gone straight home. Field said that he was dressed in a dark grey double breasted coat with grey flannel trousers.

And he was adamant: 'I did not cross the Crumbles at any time either on Thursday or Friday.'

Gray's account is similar. He mentions the visit to Pevensey Castle on the Thursday afternoon; the meeting with Maud Baxter; the ice cream after the return to Eastbourne. After a wash-up at his house they had called for a drink at the Albion, they had gone to the Hippodrome after which they had had another drink at the Albion.

There are some inconsistencies here. Neither man mentions pre-theatre drinks at the Albemarle. Gray mentions the Albion. Were these deliberate errors and omissions?

On the Friday, Gray says that he and Field spent the morning on the seafront and the afternoon and evening at cinemas. Here his account accords with Field's.

He ends his statement with a firm assertion: 'I have never been over the Crumbles in my life. I was dressed in navy blue on Thursday and Friday. I was wearing a trilby hat on Thursday.'

But there were witnesses to his wearing a grey suit on the Thursday lunchtime and in the afternoon.

And neither man mentioned Irene Munro.

Chief Inspector Mercer sought out Maud Baxter. What had she to say? Would she make a statement?

Willingly, Maud said. The men were practically strangers to her, she said. Some time after eight o'clock on Thursday evening, she met them near the Wish Tower. She'd never spoken to them before. She told them her name, said that she was a scullery maid at a house in St John's Road. She was really from Colchester, she told them.

On Sunday 22nd August and on the following day, she met them again. They all talked about the murder which had so gripped the town. She remembered that one of them told her that they had been to Pevensey on the previous Thursday and also that they had been in an ice cream shop.

But no, she told Chief Inspector Mercer, she did not go out with the men on the Thursday afternoon. How could she when the first time she spoke to them was on the Thursday evening? And, Maud Baxter said, she had never been to Pevensey Castle.

When later Mercer told Field that Miss Baxter denied being with him on the Thursday afternoon, he replied, 'I must have been mistaken about the young woman but I swear I was at Pevensey on Thursday.' But he was not. Nor was Gray. They did not get as far as Pevensey on the Thursday. But they were at the castle with Irene on the Wednesday.

During their two days in police custody, the men's houses were searched. In Field's house they found the walking stick with the carved bulldog head. He swore he had not carried it on the Thursday. But wasn't he in the bar with it? Hadn't Gray held it up, made the joke about giving his dog a biscuit? No, that was weeks before, Field said.

Mercer believed the witnesses who mentioned seeing the walking stick on the Thursday. So why did Field deny carrying it? It must be significant. Hadn't Dr Adams said 'a broad stick may have done it?' Hadn't Dr Cadman noticed injuries 'made with an instrument which pierced the roof of the mouth?' Mercer was convinced that Field's denial was proof that he had the murderers of Irene Munro before him. But there was insufficient evidence to hold them.

On their release from the cells the two men were elated by their experience. Again in the Albemarle, they were excited, triumphant, boastful. They had been locked up 'for that Crumbles turn-out', they told a pal, but they had been let out. The police had no evidence.

Some nights later Gray was in the Albemarle, sitting alone in the private bar. The barmaid Dorothy came through with the newspaper to show him the latest news about the murder. A new witness had come forward to help the police. A sailor.

And Gray grabs the newspaper from her hand and scans the page. Another witness? What does it say? Poor Billy Gray. Poor, totally illiterate Billy Gray stands up and still clutching the paper leaves the bar. Looking for Field.

After going back to his ship, William Putland had seen a picture of the murdered girl in the newspaper. He was in no doubt about it. It was the girl he'd seen the previous Thursday at the Crumbles with the two men he and Wells had followed. Unsure what to do, he did nothing for four days. But finally he spoke to his commanding officer. By Thursday 2nd September, William Putland was in front of Chief Inspector Mercer. Two days later, Saturday, at a seafront coffee stall, he identified Field by his 'tidy nose', flattened like a boxer's. That evening Jack Field and Billy Gray were taken back into custody.

The adjourned inquest on Irene Munro was resumed on 6th September. After several hearings a verdict of Wilful Murder was brought against Field and Gray. A similar verdict came from the Magistrates Court at Hailsham where both men resolutely denied responsibility for the murder. 'I think it is about time some of you knew what you were doing for we have been kept here for 16 or 17 days,' Field said. 'We were pulled up once and detained for two days and we made a statement as to where we were. That statement was proved correct and we were released and now we are detained again on that statement. You have got no evidence against us at all. Mr Mercer said he had a sailor to identify us. I have never seen him and neither has my friend. We have been up before a woman and about twelve men but none of them have identified us.'

The trial, beginning on 13th December and lasting for five days, took place at Sussex Assizes in Lewes County Hall before Mr Justice Avory. Gray comes out of the court proceedings as a particularly stupid man, shiftless, vicious and indelibly dishonest.

While Field was a young man with a poor record, at least he had the virtue of coherence.

Even before the trial Billy Gray had severely damaged his own case and by association, Field's case. While in Maidstone prison awaiting trial he had tried to suborn two prisoners.

Archibald Darrington, remanded for stealing a bicycle at Eastbourne, told how Gray asked him to say that they were together on the afternoon of the murder. Later he tried to persuade Darrington to say that he saw a sailor and a girl together on the road to Pevensey on that same afternoon. He wanted Darrington to say that when he returned along the same way later he saw the sailor alone.

Then there was the other prisoner, Smith. 'They've got me because of my clothes but they can't prove it,' Gray told Smith. 'I was with the girl almost up to an hour before she was killed. But that does not prove I done it. The worst of it is a sailor says he saw me and the girl.'

On a later occasion Gray – and he sounds hopeless, thrashing around for someone to stand by him – asked Smith to take a message to Field. 'Tell my mate to say that we did not know the girl and had never seen her. Say we were at the circus.'

All this time Gray could not take his mind off the case. He needed to talk about it. There was a dreadful, telling conversation with Smith which was later reported in court. When Smith had asked Gray how the murder was done, he had told him that a heavy stone was dropped on her head.

One vital issue in the trial related to the timing of Irene Munro's death. There was considerable scientific argument about the speed of the coagulation of blood, the cooling of corpses and the rate at which rigor mortis sets in. If, as Dr Cadman suggested, Irene died possibly late on the Thursday night, then the alibi of the accused seemed strong enough to free them.

But Mr Justice Avory's summing-up homed in on one particular feature of the case that must have already nagged away at the minds of the jury. 'Why,' he asked, 'did the two prisoners arrange between themselves to set up a false alibi as to the afternoon of the 19th unless they knew that the murder had been committed in the afternoon?'

That is about the nub of it.

On the fifth day of their trial, both men were found guilty of Wilful Murder. The jury did, however, put in a recommendation for mercy. There had been no premeditation, they said.

On Monday 17th January Field and Gray appeared at the Court of Criminal Appeal. Now both men had made new statements, each accusing the other of the murder.

Field stated that they had met Irene on the Wednesday and were with her for much of the afternoon and evening. They had visited Pevensey again on the Thursday afternoon. Field formed the opinion that Irene wished to be with Gray and not with him and so he had left them.

On the way back to Eastbourne, he had met Gray who told him that he had had a row with the girl and that she had gone home. That evening, at the Albemarle, Field asked him suddenly where he had got his money. Gray had replied angrily, 'Shut up and mind your own business. I'm paying for the drinks and that is all that concerns you.'

On the Saturday morning, according to Field, Gray admitted that the girl had said something he did not like and that he had punched her. She had lain unconscious for ten minutes or so and, in a panic, he had covered her with shingle. If Field had not left him with the girl, he said, this would never have happened. It was at this point, Field claimed, that they worked out their alibi. He said he would do his best for Gray and said that if Gray were arrested, he would tell the police that they had been to Pevensey together. In turn, Billy Gray had told him that if anything went wrong and Field were arrested and convicted, he would own up to what had happened.

Then the Appeal Court received information from a hitherto confidential report by Sir Bernard Spilsbury, the pathologist, who had examined the body of Irene Munro. Spilsbury had made the observation: 'Probably survived for short time – might have been half an hour but would be unconscious all the time.' Now Field told the court that Gray had confessed to burying the girl alive.

But why, Field was asked, should he protect such a man? Out of friendship, Field said. And he did not call upon Gray to clear him after the trial because they had been recommended to mercy. He was willing to go to prison so that Gray might return to his wife when his term had expired.

Gray now presented an entirely new slant to events. Field was lying, he said. Field was the murderer.

Gray said that after their visit to the Albemarle on the Thursday afternoon, Field went to Pevensey but he went home. He did not see Field again until he called for him in the early evening.

Then on the day of their conviction and sentence, when they were being moved to Wandsworth prison and were waiting in the stationmaster's room at Lewes station for a connection to London, Field confessed to him in whispers how he had murdered her.

Gray said that after they left each other at 10.30 pm on the Thursday night, Field told him that he met Irene in the street asking the way to her lodgings. She was lost and so he showed her the way. They had walked to the Crumbles. Then there had been a quarrel and Field had hit her. She fell down unconscious and he landed more blows which finished her off.

Then, having made this confession in the waiting room, Field had told Gray, 'You know nothing about it. You were at your own home when I did it.' He went on to say, 'Leave everything to me. I will do my best to free you.'

But there was a lack of conviction about Gray's whole sorry tale.

On 18th January, the appeals of both men were dismissed. Defence counsel Marshall Hall, never a vindictive man, would confide to a friend that he hoped both men would swing.

On 1st February a reprieve was denied and three days later Jack Field and Billy Gray were hanged together at Wandsworth. Neither man made a last-minute confession.

So then, what did happen on the Crumbles that chilly August Thursday afternoon? Why was a 17 year old girl killed by men she believed to be her friends? Robbery? She had only about £2 in her purse. Enough for a few glasses of decent beer and the odd packet of Turkish fags. And maybe a little left over to repay some petty debts. Sex? There was no sign of any attempt to interfere with her sexually. The motive for this brutal murder, so callous, so devoid of human feeling, still mystifies. Was it planned? Did Field and Gray know when they met earlier in the afternoon that they were going to kill Irene Munro?

They never said.

GREATER THAN GOD?

──────────❁──────────

'Can anyone be greater than God?' the Sunday School teacher asks her infant group.

And back comes the unhesitating answer. 'Mr Bottomley, miss.'

Things had certainly changed since the great man turned up at Upper Dicker. First he bought an old country cottage which he transformed into a vast sprawling brick-built mansion that he called The Dicker. The place just grew and grew. Now there was a large household staff, most of them from the village, required especially at weekends when Mr Bottomley invited down all his pals from London, sometimes as many as thirty staying there.

There was a huge artificial lake in the grounds now and tennis courts too. There was even talk of Bottomley building a private racecourse, for racing was his passion. His horses were trained by Mr Batho at Alfriston. And, they say, he gambled in thousands, and at race meetings he placed bets in the hundreds of thousands.

Local people did not begrudge him his extravagances – champagne and kippers for breakfast, would you believe it? – for he was such a generous man. He had rebuilt the labourers' cottages in the village. Sometimes he would even pay off the rent arrears of local people in need. And there were the village fêtes and the celebrations for the old Queen's Diamond Jubilee and the Coronation of Edward VII. These were lavish affairs. Nobody in the village had ever before experienced anything like the summer fairs or Christmas parties that Mr Bottomley laid on.

Then he went away for five years – to prison, as a matter of fact – and you can understand how when he came back they welcomed him with such enthusiasm. They turned out in large numbers to cheer him, their benefactor, even calling on the Hailsham Prize

Band to play outside the house, and they raised the Union Jack as fitting for the Great Patriot.

Not that the local gentry had ever warmed to him. Too common. And his wife, Eliza, she was just an unreconstructed little cockney, dropping her aitches all over the place. No, it was the working folk with whom he always had most in common.

Even though Horatio Bottomley was a scoundrel, you wouldn't have expressed that sentiment in Upper Dicker.

The thing is that he needn't have been such a villain. Just like other very able men – like Nicholas Hoogstraten, like Dr John Drewe, his companions in these pages – he could have made his way in the world without jiggery-pokery; he could have made a permanent mark in the House of Commons; he could have been a first-class journalist and newspaper owner. He need not have been such an unmitigated crook.

His mother, Elizabeth Holyoake, was a member of an influential family of Radical politicians. It seemed natural when, as an MP, Bottomley espoused several enlightened causes. But his father … well, that does leave us with something of a problem. Was it really the foreman tailor, William Bottomley, who spent much of his life in insane asylums? Or was his father Charles Bradlaugh, the Radical MP? Nothing is certain, save that Bottomley resembled Bradlaugh, had the same powerful skill with words.

But with both parents dead young Horatio was in an orphanage from the age of 10, leaving at 14 in 1874 to make his fortune armed with only a basic education. At the age of 15 he was working for a solicitor who was often drunk and whose managing clerk was dishonest. From them or despite them he learnt much that was wrong and little that was right, but he picked up a useful knowledge of the law. Later he worked in the law courts as a reporter and shorthand writer. What a learning ground this proved to be for a sharp lad with an eye on the main chance. At this time his interest in politics and social matters began.

In 1884 at the age of 24 he founded his first newspaper, *The Hackney Hansard*, which reported the proceedings of the local political debating society or 'Parliament'. This was successful in an age when working men were but recently enfranchised. He then extended the Hansards to other parts of London and later he started various magazines relating to commerce, shipping, and local government. What flair, what energy in a young man of such modest educational opportunity.

Then came the *Financial Times* which he began in 1888. Was there no end to the young tycoon's progress? Well, yes, there was. For he managed to overstretch himself. As with most of Bottomley's financial dealings there was always a shortage of ready cash, always a need to support his extravagant lifestyle – wine, women, song and of course, gambling – always the inclination to help himself from what in reality belonged to shareholders.

In 1893 he was charged with conspiring to obtain money from the shareholders of his company, the Hansard Union. He had recommended that they buy some companies for £325,000. But these had already been bought at knock-down prices by Bottomley's own front man for £238,000. So the poor old shareholders forked out the cash and the balance for the most part went into the pockets of Bottomley and some of his directors.

And listen to this. He was widely expected to go to gaol yet he was acquitted. Against some of the finest advocates in the land Bottomley, who had never sat a law examination in his life, defended himself in court. So impressed was he by the performance that Mr Justice Hawkins told the jury that 'nobody could doubt the honesty of his motives.' After the case the judge sent for him and advised him to go to the Bar.

Certainly in the many cases where Bottomley represented himself he was majestic, knowing and instantly recalling every fact, every figure – and that included every phoney fact, every false figure.

And even though he had made the Hansard Union bankrupt within two years and there was over £600,000 which could not be accounted for, the 33 year old was still regarded as a financial genius. So the so-called 'best lay-lawyer' in the land stayed in the City where the money was. He might still be bankrupt but he had ways of dealing with creditors.

Bottomley always employed artful – some would say devoted and dishonest – associates. After the Hansard case he sent out these agents to his creditors. They told these already desperately deceived people that they represented a syndicate trying to reach an accommodation with Bottomley. Trouble was, they would say, he had very little money and there was very little chance of recovering anything. They would offer a minimal sum – they could do no better, they would say with some regret – and very many were glad to get at least some tiny recompense. Better than nothing.

Small wonder then that as a bankrupt Bottomley seemed so resilient. Within two years of the Hansard debacle, he was once more a man of substantial wealth. And so it was to go on throughout his life, despite all of the suspicions that he was hugely dishonest and profligate. But, as was said at the time, Horatio Bottomley had two brains, one which linked up with his tongue and the other which thought while he talked.

In the 1890s gold was discovered in Western Australia. And the speculators moved in. It was just the kind of pool for sharks to swim in. And there was Bottomley, swimming with the rest. From 1893, on borrowed money, he promoted mining companies. Sadly though for many of those who invested there was often little in the way of profit. They would receive one very encouraging dividend, enough to make them dig deeper into their capital and to persuade their friends and relatives to put money into Australian gold. But then all too often the companies were liquidated and investors received regretful letters explaining the reasons in some or other plausible manner. Bottomley for his part, however, made a fortune. The only mining appears to have been from the shareholders' portfolios.

A letter to one of his fellow directors, written in the late 1890s, gives some indication of the bait laid for gullible investors in gold. 'My Dear Harry,' he writes, 'What on earth have you done with our nugget – the one we used to show to shareholders in the old days? I've got hold of a very promising client. All he wants is a sight of the stuff.'

He spent a lifetime cozening the gullible. At shareholders' meetings he played the same tune to those who were concerned that their investments were now worthless. Look, he'd tell them, this short, fat, twinkly-eyed man, we have hit bad times. But we're overcoming these short term difficulties, he'd say. The company

Horatio Bottomley

has turned round and we're on the road to recovery. There are good times coming, he'd tell them, the prospects are rosy. Personally, he would say, he would like to pay a good dividend immediately but he would indicate that the company's directors – more wise and level-headed than he, he would imply – were advising just a little caution for the moment. But, and this was his tip, he'd recommend immediate purchase of the company's shares while the price was still low. And at each point he made, there'd be a rumble of 'Hear, hears' and applause from paid supporters all round the hall.

In 1906 Bottomley became Liberal MP for South Hackney. He was a wonderful performer on the hustings, witty and optimistic, the working man's friend. And such jokes. What a card.

'Is the candidate in favour of mixed bathing for the unemployed?' he is asked at one meeting.

Back comes the cheeky chappie: 'I am quite unable to consider the possibility of their being unemployed under such conditions.'

And they loved him. He was one of them. Even dressed like them in a plain grey suit. At least he did when he sought working class votes. In the City, he wore a topper and had a fur coat over his frock coat, whilst down at The Dicker he wore the tweeds of a country gentleman. Master of spin, Mr Bottomley. He spins and his observers get dizzy.

And in Parliament he's all for better Old Age Pensions and a relaxation of the licensing laws; why can't shops open on Sundays, he asks, and what about putting a tax on betting and finding some money from share certificates and taxes on employers? In the abstract he's all for the poor and the old.

At this time he has also introduced *John Bull*, the magazine for which he's best known. It's a model for today's tabloids. 'If you read it in *John Bull* – it is so', runs the slogan. And if you believe that you can believe anything.

There are all sort of exposures: disappearing vicars; dubious massage parlours; Aleister Crowley, who is described as 'scum'; a tale about a Worthing workman and a 'photo fiend'. The French, he tells us, are 'corrupt, tyrannical, bloodthirsty, sycophantic, unmannerly, treacherous and lecherous.' And the Germans, well ...

Inevitably there were court cases involving the aggrieved and, as ever, Bottomley defended himself, playing his usual role of the ordinary man trying to make a living.

John Bull ran all kinds of competitions with the promise of handsome cash prizes. In 1913 the magazine ran a Derby sweepstake with a first prize of £15,000. And, oh, how the money rolled in.

The following year there was a problem. There was a prize of £5,000 on the Grand National. Some carelessness somewhere – it was won by an outsider who was not one of Bottomley's employees. But the Derby lottery of that year – first prize £250,000 – was won by 'Madame Glukad, a blind lady of Toulouse' who just happened to be the sister of one of Bottomley's henchmen. In the end, she received only £250.

And there were always other shady enterprises: for instance, the Basingstoke Canal scheme, 35 miles long but dry. Still it loosened some purses.

Despite all of this finagling and all of the money-making schemes, in 1912 Bottomley was declared bankrupt in a case brought by Prudential Assurance. Where did the money go? Well, he had rich tastes. That was it. Champagne, horses, ladies ... oh yes, ladies, set up in flats in the West End.

The upshot was that he lost the case, was declared bankrupt and, to his genuine regret, was obliged to retire from Parliament.

But he reinvented himself. The First World War broke out and he jumped on the patriotic bandwagon. He appeared all over the country exhorting young men to volunteer for the army, to fight for King and Country. And he was powerfully effective.

Naturalised Germans living in Britain had their windows smashed as a consequence of his virulent speeches. Dachshunds were stoned and kicked. German sailors, Bottomley said, should be hanged or allowed to drown and no German prisoners should be taken. 'If by chance you should discover one day in a restaurant that you are being served by a German waiter,' he told *John Bull* readers, 'throw the soup in his face.'

In 1917 Bottomley visited the front line and met 'the boys who are actually fighting'. He wrote articles entitled 'What Haig Told Me' and, after visiting the Grand Fleet, 'What Admiral Beatty

Told Me'. No wonder, with such a heroic figure at its head, *John Bull* became 'The Tommy's Bible.' But it was not public knowledge that Bottomley asked generous expenses for his patriotic visits nor that for his articles in the *Sunday Pictorial* about the poor soldiers he was paid £7,800 per annum.

After the war, no longer a bankrupt, back he came into Parliament. It seemed that he always bounced back.

Then from this high point of immense popularity came the sudden end of Bottomley. In 1919, the last great swindle, the *John Bull* Victory Bond Club was launched. The aim was to enable poor people to take part in the government's Victory Bond Scheme. But the government's bonds cost £5 each. Bottomley's scheme was simple. He bought government bonds and for £1 subscribers could buy a fifth of one share with a promise of other cash prizes. From this scheme the subscribers would be given an annual interest on their investment. Bottomley's plan was so successful that, at one point, he was receiving £1,000,000 a day. But the interest on the money which rolled in did not go to the investors. Bottomley had his own debts to pay off.

In 1922 he was charged with 'fraudulently converting to his own use sums of money entrusted to him by members of the public.' At the end of the trial, at which as ever he defended himself, he was sentenced to seven years. Sixty-two years old and the high roller went to prison at last.

'Sewing, Bottomley?' asked a prison visitor, seeing him working on the mail bags.

'Reaping,' he responded, never at a loss for a ready reply.

And then, after five years, he returns to Upper Dicker, Hailsham Prize Band and all. And tries to make a start again. Sets up a newspaper but it fails. Appears on stage for three weeks at the Windmill Theatre between the red-nosed comedian and the strippers, tries to tell the audience interesting tales from his life and fails. He is a forgotten man.

The days of the great swindler, the old charmer, are over.

BIBLIOGRAPHY

———— ✿ ————

David Briffett, *The Acid Bath Murders* Field Place Press 1988
Edward Greeno, *War on the Underworld* John Long 1960
Edward T. Hart, *Britain's Godfather* True Crime Library 1993
Alan Hyman, *The Rise and fall of Horatio Bottomley* Cassell
  1972
Arthur La Bern, *Haigh: The Mind of a Murderer* W.H. Allen 1973
Lenny McLean and Peter Gerrard, *The Guv'nor* Blake 1998
James Morton, *Gangland* Warner 1994
Robert Murphy, *Smash and Grab* Faber and Faber 1992
Julian Symons, *Horatio Bottomley* Cressett 1955

The author has also consulted a wide variety of newspapers and
magazines, both local and national.